# Finding Hope

# Finding Hope:
## My Journey Out Of Darkness

*Linda Keehn*

XULON PRESS

Xulon Press
2301 Lucien Way #415
Maitland, FL 32751
407.339.4217
www.xulonpress.com

© 2020 by Linda Keehn

All rights reserved solely by the author. The author guarantees all contents are original and do not infringe upon the legal rights of any other person or work. No part of this book may be reproduced in any form without the permission of the author. The views expressed in this book are not necessarily those of the publisher.

Unless otherwise indicated, all Scripture quotations are from *The Nelson Study Bible*, New King James Version, copyright © 1997 by Thomas Nelson Publishers.

Printed in the United States of America

Paperback ISBN-13: 978-1-6322-1320-4
Ebook ISBN-13: 978-1-6322-1321-1

# Dedication

My primary reason for writing this book is to respond to the prompting of the Holy Spirit: tell others of the hope that is available in Jesus Christ. My changed life is evidence of the hope that is found by having a personal relationship with Him. My secondary reason for writing this book is to help you find hope through the power of the Holy Spirit, by either learning from my mistakes or by being motivated to carefully consider your life's choices and make sure you are heading in the right direction on your spiritual journey. Remember, experience is a good teacher, and fools learn by no other, so learn from my mistakes rather than having to learn from your own.

This book is dedicated to my two sons, Bill and Justin, who suffered consequences of my choices. My deepest appreciation goes to my husband, Roger, for his love and support throughout thirty-two years of shared trials. My sincere thanks go to my spiritual mentor and faithful friend, Rich.

# Table of Contents

Introduction . . . . . . . . . . . . . . . . . . . . . . . . . . . . . . . . ix
Chapter 1. Something Missing . . . . . . . . . . . . . . . . . . 1
Chapter 2. Darkness Descending . . . . . . . . . . . . . . 10
Chapter 3. Hope Dawning . . . . . . . . . . . . . . . . . . . . 18
Chapter 4. Power to Change . . . . . . . . . . . . . . . . . . 23
Chapter 5. Relationships Matter . . . . . . . . . . . . . . . . 28
Chapter 6. Overcoming Trials . . . . . . . . . . . . . . . . . . 38
Chapter 7. Spiritual Battlefield . . . . . . . . . . . . . . . . . 46
Chapter 8. Rejecting the Lies . . . . . . . . . . . . . . . . . . 56
Chapter 9. Ample Provision . . . . . . . . . . . . . . . . . . . 64
Chapter 10. Daily Strength . . . . . . . . . . . . . . . . . . . 79
Chapter 11. Peaceful Presence . . . . . . . . . . . . . . . . . 93
Chapter 12. A Fresh Perspective . . . . . . . . . . . . . . 103
Chapter 13. Delighting in Blessings Found . . . . 114
Reader Reflections . . . . . . . . . . . . . . . . . . . . . . . . . 127

# Introduction

AS MY RETIREMENT DATE APPROACHED, I REALIZED NEW doors were about to open for me. The forty- to sixty-hour work weeks I had known for eight years were ending; my time would soon be my own. How would I stay busy? What meaningful contribution might I still make? What would I do that I had postponed for so long? My thoughts immediately turned to "the book" I had planned to write but had put off time and time again. The first two thirds of my life had been shrouded in darkness, succumbing to alcohol addiction and a lifestyle of meaningless sexual encounters, yearning for something but not knowing what, labeling myself a failure and loser time and time again, seeing myself as not lovable and worthy. The downward spiral led to a bottomless pit filled with shame, regret, broken marriages, abandoned children, and the loss of hope. When I reached the end of my own abilities and finally realized there was nothing I could do to fix what was wrong with me, I knew my life was out of control and that I would face an early death if something didn't change.

For many of us, religion can be a turn-off, especially if we have not attended church regularly, have had a bad experience with religious people, or simply don't want to feel pressured regarding faith. I understand the hesitation, even resistance, because that described me for the first forty-four years of my life. It took that long for me to turn to what I had seen as the "last resort" for so long. If things are not going right in your life— you are feeling trapped, lost, desperate, hopeless—and seeking relief, looking for a way out, or wanting something better— there may be an answer in my story for you. Please continue reading!

Discover the things that contributed to my sense of despair and addiction. What has caused your loss of hope or reliance on alcohol, drugs, pornography, or some other means of escape? Learn how I went from a position of denying God to one of trusting in and relying on

*Finding Hope*

Him. What is it that is holding you back? What you are about to read is my testimony—one life changed by the power of Jesus Christ. See how lives are changed, hope is restored, and faith grows during the trials of life. If you find yourself walking in darkness as I once did, won't you give my "last resort" a try?

My desire is that this is not just a book about my life, but that it opens a door for you to look at your own journey. Allow me to come alongside of you and help you examine your life, your decisions, your relationships, and the lies you have believed and encourage you to make choices that will help you find the hope and assurance that I have found. So, at the end of my story you will find Reader Reflections, a guide that provides questions, topics, and/or action steps for your consideration to help you find hope, a changed life, and a relationship that will lift you up to heights you never dreamed possible!

# Chapter 1

## Something Missing

I WAS BORN IN A SMALL NEW ENGLAND TOWN, THE only daughter of a carpenter and a homemaker. My closest childhood friend was a first cousin, the daughter of my mom's twin sister, who lived about five miles away from my home. We lived in a rural area of rolling hills with apple trees, blueberry fields, wildlife, and birds. The beauty of brilliant stars in the dark sky at night, a wildflower blooming alongside a small stream, or an occasional evening walk with my dad were things that brought me joy. Our modest frame home was simple but comfortable, with the inviting scent of fresh-baked cookies, hot apple pie, or fresh bread wafting from my mom's kitchen when I arrived home after school. My dad was a hard worker, taking small carpentry projects outside of his regular job to supplement our family income in addition to devoting hours of volunteer work on his parents' nearby farm. When not working, my father spent time hunting, fishing, and drinking with several of his brothers who lived along the same country road we did. They swapped tales as they drank and seemed to find solace in their hours together. One year, Dad made hard apple cider in wooden kegs stored in the damp, dark, dirt-floored basement of our home. Night after night dad and his brothers gathered in the dimly lit, cramped space enjoying the potent drink. It was a good time for the men. Dad's many commitments resulted in there being little time available for him to spend with mom and me. I felt lonely and left out. It felt like Dad's work, what he did to help out on his parents' farm, and drinking with his brothers all mattered more than me.

Alcohol consumption was a part of daily living in our home, something I thought was normal in other homes as well. It was common for my parents to pull off the main road during the after-work drive from the city and stop for a drink before continuing on to our rural home. I considered alcohol to be a treat, something people used to relax after a hard day of work or to celebrate, but also sometimes a crutch to get through tough times. I had my own favorite treats during the stops: pistachio nuts in the shell or beef jerky. At a young age I learned dependency, using food as a treat, a reward when things were going well or a crutch to make me feel better when things did not go well.

Mom was a full-time homemaker until my high school years when she and her sister began doing seasonal office work in the adjacent city. During the time she and I had alone prior to that, I learned cooking, baking, sewing, and general home management by watching and helping her. Mom's braised pot roast, with rich brown gravy and vegetables was the best! Her skill creating things with yeast (bread, prune pockets, and cinnamon rolls) was amazing. The high point of the week was grocery shopping in the adjacent city and a visit with my mom's parents afterwards. Mom always seemed happiest spending time with her parents and sister. The visits were something I also looked forward to. My cousin and I had the undivided attention of our grandparents. They were interested in what I was doing in school, they showed affection with their hugs, and they always had snacks and beverages ready to share during the visits. Their home was inviting and comfortable, with no furniture or areas off-limits to their grandchildren. If the visits were long enough, my cousin and I were able to clamp on roller skates and circle around in the paved basement while the grown-ups talked upstairs. I felt welcome in my grandparents' city home. With them, I always felt safe and loved.

The local grammar school was located in the town center, so I rode the school bus five days a week to attend classes. My contact with children my own age was mainly during school hours due to the rural nature of the community and no neighbor children in my age range living nearby. My temperament was not always conducive to making friends even when I was with children my own age. My cousin was of a petite build during our years in grade school, looking frail compared to me, with my more sturdy build. One day on the playground she didn't do what I wanted her to do during a game, and I slapped her hard across the cheek. Our relationship was strained for a while, with me feeling guilty and her feeling hurt. I knew I had been in the wrong but didn't know how to make things right. I was afraid I was going to lose my best friend. There was a strain between us for days that faded gradually as I treated her with kindness. The only time I recall having a birthday party with friends at my home, something wasn't going the way I wanted, and I stormed off from the group in a fit of temper. The other children continued with the party activities, having a good time, while I brooded in a corner by myself. My angry behavior had little effect on them, but it distanced me from friends and what could have been a fun day. I began to see there was a cost associated with my anger.

Even in grade school there was a sense of something being different about me; the desires I had for connection, acceptance, and approval went unmet. Being a bully and trying to control things to make them go my way didn't help me make friends. I spent hours alone playing in the apple orchard behind our house, climbing trees, and running in the tall field grass. Sometimes I roamed into the nearby woods where I pretended the fallen trees were furniture and served imaginary food, chunks of decomposing wood that I pretended was chicken, to my invisible guests. When the blueberry crop was ready for summer harvest, I would walk up a wooded, hilly path to reach the berries, eat as I picked, and then return home with my prize to share with my parents. I enjoyed the time I spent alone in this manner. Being in nature and using my imagination in this way was refreshing and energizing to me. My parents' delight in the fresh berries I brought to them helped meet my need for acceptance and approval. It was years before I began to understand that a natural inclination toward introversion, finding refreshment away from gatherings of people, was involved in my sense of not belonging and the feeling of being different.

In the spring and summer months my mother tended a flower garden by the side of our house, with fragrant lilies of the valley and gardenias included in her list of favorites. When vegetables ripened in the larger garden plot, Mom canned pickles, tomatoes, and relishes for us to enjoy during the fall and winter months. On a few occasions, Dad and I got to sit on the large flat rock near the middle of grandpa's blueberry field just before sunset in the summer. As the sun lowered in the sky, we gazed out at the surrounding hills as if surveying the entire world before us. Those times, when I had Dad's undivided attention, were so special. On a rare spring outing along a clear stream, I spied a pale pink flower growing just beyond my reach. Dad hoisted me atop his shoulders and waded through the boggy area so I could retrieve my treasure, a beautiful, delicate lady's slipper. Another time we walked in the cold along the country road leading to my grandparent's home, looking up at the colorful lights of the aurora borealis displayed across the night sky. Its beauty seemed to take my breath away. It was during these grammar school years that my love of nature took seed and grew over time. My hunger for special time with my dad also grew as I had these rare positive experiences with him. It seemed I could never get enough of his attention.

My father's family was large, with several uncles, an aunt and my grandparents all living near us and the remainder of his family living in adjacent small towns or cities. There were many grandchildren, enough that my poor grandma often had trouble recalling my name when I visited her at the large farmhouse next door where she and Grandpa lived. The two older girl cousins who lived near us seemed to get most of the attention. I felt left out and unimportant, not really welcomed, so I spent little time there. My mom's family was small, with only two grandchildren, so my cousin and I both received ample attention when we visited our grandparents in the adjacent city where my mom had been raised. I looked forward to overnight visits there with my cousin. We would snuggle in our twin beds and talk long after bedtime, giggling at the sound of Grandpa's loud snoring coming from a room at one end of the hall. Sometimes we made so much noise that Grandma had to get out of bed and come ask us to settle down and be quiet. Grandpa always praised me for good grades on my report card, and he funded the "tooth fairy" at every opportunity. He liked to dunk ginger snaps in his cup of black coffee, and I looked forward to dunking gingersnaps with him whenever I spent time visiting with him and grandma. At Thanksgiving and Christmas, we both enjoyed eating minced pie with sage cheese, a pleasure not shared by many others at the family gatherings. There was a sense of connection, acceptance, and approval from those grandparents, where good memories still linger from the time spent with them.

My concept of what marriage, family, and relationships should be like grew from the seed that was planted as I spent time in my grandparents' home. I saw a man and woman who loved each other, displaying kindness and mutual respect. If there were harsh words exchanged or voices raised in anger, I never heard them. My grandpa had been a hard worker all his life, providing a good home for Grandma and their two daughters until they married. My grandparents were responsible people, keeping their home and yard in good order. Together they grew flowers to beautify the yard and attract birds and butterflies in season. I loved to spend time in their yard in the summertime when things were in full bloom. They had friends and demonstrated hospitality throughout the year, not just at the holidays. My grandpa's mother lived with them until she died in her mid-nineties. I longed for what I saw in my grandparents' relationship with each other and envisioned having a home like theirs someday.

As a child, my primary Christmas focus was on presents, and I was never disappointed. As an only child and one of only two grandchildren on my mother's side of the family, I did not have to compete with others or share things the way children in larger families do. My cousin and I usually received the same gifts, with only individual color preferences resulting in slight differences in the clothing items. Each year we looked forward to receiving a new doll, the large, boxed beauties that lined the shelves in the toy departments at that time of year. The year I turned twelve, I received a bride doll, the culmination of the doll years, somewhat a rite of passage for a girl. It was customary for us to put up a freshly cut tree in our house a little while before Christmas, with my mom and me responsible for the decorating while Dad spent time with his brothers. Each year something went wrong during the process, and there was tension: the tree started to topple over, a prized ornament fell and broke, or an argument broke out among the alcohol-drinking grownups gathered there. After dinner on Christmas Eve I received permission to start opening gifts that were stacked high in a pile in front of me. Once the frenzy of opening gifts ended, there was a letdown feeling, a kind of emptiness. Santa, Rudolph, and "Jingle Bells" were all part of the holiday celebration, but it was all anticlimactic once the gifts had been opened. My family did not attend church or include the birth of Christ in any way as part of our Christmas celebration. At Easter time my mother and I dyed hard-boiled eggs and decorated them together. I loved dipping the eggs in the colored water, sometimes mixing and matching to create new and different shades.

*Finding Hope*

On Easter morning she hid the eggs in various places—outside if the weather allowed or inside if it was stormy or too cold. Springtime could be unpredictable in New England, with patches of snow some years lingering into May. Chocolate and marshmallow bunnies, fake straw in woven baskets, and pretty dresses are what I remember about Easter in my home. I don't recall Dad taking part in the annual ritual or there being any focus on the religious significance of Easter. The pleasure of the holidays, the excitement at opening packages, and searching for eggs was temporary. When the last box was opened and the last egg found, there was nothing more; there was no lasting joy in my holidays.

The memories of my high school years are not pleasant. The need I had developed earlier for acceptance, approval, and love left me vulnerable to advances by a married man. I was curious and experiencing the myriad emotional and physical changes that come with puberty, feeling flattered by the man's attention even though I knew at some level that what I was doing was wrong. I lost my virginity to him in my early teens and was involved in a short-term sexual relationship with him. Mom and I had never had a talk about sex, the benefits of abstinence, or the emotional costs of sexual activity outside of marriage. I remember at some time hearing an adult in the family say, "All you have to do is keep your legs crossed." Even if I had received better instruction, I doubt it would have kept me from engaging in the sexual behavior, as focused on finding love and feeling special as I was. I did not know what to expect the first time I had intercourse and was frightened by the pain and the sight of my own blood. My cousin was still my best friend, and she was the only one who knew what was happening. When my sexual involvement came to light, my dad took immediate action and contacted law enforcement. My emotions fluctuated wildly, between panic one moment and a sense of relief the next. Panic that the affair was out in the open and there was no putting that genie back in the bottle; fear of what my dad might do to the man, yet relief that I was no longer living a secret life and hiding things from my parents. I had been living a lie—sneaking around, skipping school, changing attendance on my report card; it had been simply a matter of time before things came crashing down around me. When they did, it was at the breakfast table in our simple country home.

In a small-town word of my indiscretion spread quickly; it seemed there was no place for me to hide. It was hard for me to look people, especially my parents, in the eye throughout the criminal investigation and the court appearance that followed. It seemed like everybody was looking at me, pointing a finger, and talking about what had happened. When a pelvic exam was needed as part of the legal investigation, it was an uncle who pushed me in a wheelchair to the exam room in the local hospital. I was so embarrassed! On the first day of the trial, I dressed in a lilac-colored suit and wore high heels, wearing the best outfit I had and looking older than I really was. The prosecution team quickly directed me to dress differently the next day. The following day I wore a simple pale-yellow skirt and blouse, reflecting more appropriately my young age and suggesting the innocence lost. No matter what I wore, I still felt shame and guilt and wanted to run away and hide. I regretted what I had done and the way my behavior had impacted my family. A kind local pastor reached out to us and invited me to attend his church. I felt so unworthy and out of place in the church setting, so different from the other young people in the group I attended, that I did not participate very long. If anybody talked about Christ and the need for a personal relationship with Him during my short connection with the church, I don't recall it.

There is one positive point that stands out during my high school years: beach camping for a week with my parents. The summer I graduated we planned a family outing, the only vacation I remember us ever taking, to celebrate. We set up camp in a shaded area, with our vehicle and tent within easy walking distance of the beautiful, inviting sandy beach. We connected with other campers and enjoyed evenings around a campfire, time for reading and sunning, as well as enjoying homemade chowder from the clams my dad and the other men gathered earlier in the day. It was a wonderful week marking the end of my troubled high school years and the transition into my adult work years.

After graduation from high school I began work at a major insurance company in one of the larger cities within daily driving distance of home. The college prep classes I had taken in high school helped me score well enough to gain employment there in a department where actuaries worked. The actuaries, who excelled in math, analyzed statistics and made forecasts to help the company determine its options related to financial and pension decisions. My immediate supervisor was a man with a physical disability of both arms. He was a smart, kind manager who showed interest in me, and we eventually began to date. I felt special when we went out together. He took me to nice restaurants, fancy compared to the places I had gone with my parents. Until then having scallops and French fries in a small, local restaurant had been a real treat. With him I experienced fine dining, some ethnic cuisine, and impeccable service in attractive settings. There were cocktails and wine when we dined out, and even though I was underage for drinking, that seldom presented a problem. Being in the presence of a professional man, dressed in a suit and tie and exuding an air of confidence in his surroundings, seemed to open the door to all sorts of new opportunities for me. I felt very grown-up and very special. My need for acceptance and approval was being met.

My insecurities surfaced when it was time to meet his family. They seemed so different from me and my family. His mom, his younger sister, and a close aunt were all college graduates and professional people while nobody in my family had even attended college. My mom had graduated from high school, but my dad had not. He was self-taught in many ways and had managed to do well enough in the Army Air Corps to become an instructor in mechanics on the big bombers flown in World War II. They were city people, while we were country people, and our home was modest compared to what they were used to. It seemed our families were worlds apart, and as I made mental comparison, it felt like we did not measure up. Feelings of inferiority and inadequacy were high as I approached marriage for the first time. Jim and I were married in 1967 in a formal church ceremony, with his widowed mother, sister and brother, favorite aunt, and my parents all present for the event.

Prior to the birth of our first son in the summer of 1969, we moved to Phoenix, Arizona, where my husband began work at a small actuarial consulting firm. He still analyzed statistics as he had at the insurance company, but now he provided the service to individual clients rather than to an insurance company. Math had never been my strongest subject in school, so we had little in common when it came to his work and my interests and abilities. My mom had been upset about our move to another state, especially one on the opposite side of the country. She saw the move as my abandoning her. She had been faithful to visit her parents and spend time with them weekly and had expected that I would continue that tradition with her once I married and had a home of my own. We had never talked about her expectation, but relatives shared with me how hurt my mom was. There was little long-distance communication with her after the move to Arizona. Mom was diagnosed with cancer the following year and died before the birth of our first son. My last visit with her was on the day the doctors shared the diagnosis with her while family members gathered around her bed. Most of the family already knew there was little hope for my mom; they had been putting on false faces in their attempt to cheer her. On this day, the prognosis was still withheld from her, and I continued to show a brave face as I said goodbye to my mom for the last time. With my mom gone and no close female friends to support me during my first pregnancy, I relied on childbirth classes to guide me through the new experience. In some ways it seemed I too had been abandoned at one of life's most precious moments: cancer was the cruel enemy who took my mom before we had a chance to reconcile, before she had a chance to see her grandson.

Before our second son was born eighteen months later, we had moved from a two-bedroom apartment to a single-family residence in an area of well-maintained older homes. We settled into a routine: my husband was the financial provider and immersed in his job; I was the homemaker, maintaining our home and caring for our children. Alcohol was the connecting factor in our daily routine with cocktails or wine, sometimes both, marking the transition for both of us from work to the evening hours. Daily drinking seemed normal to me, having been raised in a home where both parents drank alcohol, sometimes in excess. It was not until many years later that I began to question my own use of alcohol and recognize that it was a problem, a serious problem!

## Chapter 2

# Darkness Descending

As a little girl I had dreamed of becoming a nurse. The white cap with a black band, what registered nurses wore in the movies and on television shows, was what I longed to have. I saw myself wearing that cap and helping people. It seemed like such a lofty calling. During my high school years, I enrolled in college prep classes so I would be prepared for further education in nursing if there was an opportunity. Over the years, I had taken in stray cats and tried to rescue fallen birds or bunnies the cats sometimes caught. If they didn't survive, I sometimes dug a grave for them and said a few words as I laid them to rest. I saw myself as a rescuer and helper. By the time I graduated from high school in 1964, the desire to continue my education had diminished. I knew the cost of higher education would be a burden to my parents, so I decided to go to work following graduation, putting my nursing dream aside for the moment. When my younger son was two, I enrolled in the local community college, taking pre-nursing classes in anticipation of completing my studies at the university level. By taking less than a fulltime course load and attending summer school sessions, I was able to care for our children and home while completing the prerequisites in the summer of 1975. My grades were good, and I graduated with highest honors. At a surface level, I wanted to be a nurse to make a difference and help people. But there was something at a deeper level, something internal, driving me to achieve, to be something more. I felt like I was my husband's wife, nothing more, as if I had no identity of my own. I thought having a nursing degree would fix that, would provide the thing that was missing so that I would finally be happy.

 I recall participating in a group activity during one of my first nursing courses at the university. Students were asked to position themselves in the room as various topics were discussed, with one side of the room representing being 100 percent in favor of a position and the opposite side being totally against it. When the topic of marital infidelity was presented, I positioned myself just a step from the wall that represented being 100 percent against it. Yet before the term had ended, I was involved in an extramarital affair. Heavy drinking and my first experience with marijuana influenced the initial encounter. I could have walked away, but I didn't. It wasn't long before my husband began asking questions, and I quickly broke down and confessed my affair. There were clandestine meetings in motels, desert dirt bike outings, and unrealistic expectations dancing in my mind. How could I possibly think that a man who had been unfaithful to his wife and child would suddenly change and be faithful and loving to me? The secret life, filled with deceit, took its toll on me. Although my husband and I attended counseling sessions, attempting to work through my infidelity, I still felt what I had done was unforgiveable; I could not forgive myself. The thought of separating my sons, of one living with me and one living with their father, was unbearable to me. We never discussed the possibility of both boys living with me. Their dad's higher education had already been acquired, and he had a good job that would provide financially for them. I was still working on a nursing degree and had no source of income. Once I completed my training, my income would be a small portion of what their dad earned. I could not imagine completing my education while raising our sons alone. A painful memory from those days is etched in my mind: I see myself standing in the doorway of my children's bedroom, watching them as they slept, with tears streaming down my face. I had put my needs and desires above the needs of my children. I had wanted to feel loved and be happy. When I didn't feel loved by my husband, when it seemed his job was the higher priority and it felt like I was taken for granted, I sought fulfillment elsewhere. I was selfish. I was a quitter. I had not communicated my needs to my spouse; I was not even sure what my needs were, and I had no idea how to begin to figure them out. I could see no way to continue in our marriage after what I had done, so I just gave up, and we divorced. I ran away from the responsibilities of motherhood as well as my marriage commitment and tried to make myself feel better by saying it would be better for my children in the long run than growing up in an unhappy marriage.

My sons lived with their dad and his mother, in the house he and I had chosen together, while I moved into an apartment and became the noncustodial parent with weekend visiting privileges. I know for a fact that classmates whispered about me, wondering how I could have left my children. The shame and unworthiness I had felt as a young teenager, when my first sexual transgression was made public, returned. I felt like such a hopeless failure! My time alone was filled with drinking to numb the pain and guilt, as well as studying so I could graduate and have the profession that I thought would save me. Suspicions and jealousy over my lover and his wife hounded me. I sometimes walked the streets at night hoping for a glimpse of their interactions. In my hopeless rage, I slashed a wall poster to shreds one night with a paring knife. My anger escaped in other ways, too: cursing, using coarse hand gestures at other drivers, and driving too fast. By Thanksgiving the affair was over. The slim hope I had held of being included with him in a holiday dinner did not come through. He was with family, and I was alone. Whatever foolish dreams I held vanished, and I was left with the reality of my foolish choices.

My greatest shame came prior to the divorce when Jim sent me off to see my dad in South Dakota where he had moved after my mom died. Having to face my dad, sharing the awful situation with him, and feeling like I was a complete loser was almost more than I could bear. I had always wanted to please my dad, to merit his approval, and to receive his love in return. I knew I had let him down, and I feared he could not love me as I was. I did not feel worthy to even be there with him in his small rental cottage. Our days were filled with small talk, some mention of the impending divorce, daily routine, and ice fishing. On a blustery, extremely cold day we ventured out for several hours of ice fishing from a little shelter on the lake. My Arizona clothing was not appropriate for the weather, so I was bundled up in layers of Dad's shirts and wore several pairs of wool socks inside a pair of his big boots. It would have been a fun adventure under different circumstances, but the unspoken words—the avoidance of my adultery and the impact on my children—hung over every moment. I had hoped he would understand me or rebuke me, be supportive or angry, but there was nothing.

I came with my shame to see my dad, and I left with my shame. It was a relief to me that my mom was not alive to see my failure.

In 1977 I graduated with a bachelor's degree in nursing and began work at a local hospital. I remarried soon after graduation, feeling incomplete without an intimate relationship and thinking marriage to the "right" person would fix everything. At that time, I thought the right person was someone who revealed tender emotions, was a bit of a dreamer, had shared dreams with me, was attentive to me, and freely showed affection toward me. The qualities I sought in a partner were almost the opposite of what I saw in my dad as I grew up and what I experienced in my first marriage. Don and I joined in matrimony with some unrealistic expectations of what a marriage partner can do or be, and our inability to meet each other's needs eventually pulled us apart. Some of the attention and behaviors that had seemed so sweet initially began to feel stifling to me over time. The poetry and songs of the dating days seemed a luxury and not helpful during tight financial times. My pragmatic style became more extreme under stress and clashed with the creative dreamer in him. I was immersed in my nursing career, focused on patient care and successful outcomes during work hours. I resented giving up a 3–11 hospital shift in a coronary care unit to accommodate his more traditional day shift. There was more traffic through the general nursing unit I transferred to during the day shift: doctors making rounds, patients going for various tests in other areas of the hospital, and daily admissions and discharges. The amount of one-on-one time with patients diminished amidst the IV and oral medications I provided to a larger number of patients, the written notes required in patient charts and being a handmaiden to the doctors as they made their rounds. The hours Don and I had together did not change much, and I was tired and cranky when I was at home, given the change in my duties at the hospital. Eventually I transferred back to the evening shift, 3–11, in the coronary care unit where I had begun. In that area of nursing I found a sense of accomplishment and satisfaction. In the coronary unit, life and death teetered on a fulcrum, trying to maintain that delicate balance. Coronary events did not fit into a nice neat box, respecting certain ages, lifestyles, or cultures. Somewhere during the years of watching monitors, starting IVs, and performing CPR, I came to realize that I, like my patients, was vulnerable. It was one thing to see an elderly patient with a long history of heart disease in the coronary unit; it was quite different to see a young woman in the last trimester of pregnancy fighting for life due to an enlarged, failing heart. Her dreams of motherhood, her hopes for her child and their future together, even their very lives were completely out of her control. One of the most difficult things I did as a coronary nurse was turning off the respirator on a female patient close to my own age after serial brain wave measurements indicated no chance of recovery. When my second marriage ended after five years, I felt like a wounded, vulnerable two-time loser. My efforts to control things, thinking I could pick the "right person" or be the "right person" had failed. My age, my health, my education held no guarantee for success in marriage. I had tried marriage twice and like a boxer in the ring, I had been knocked out both times. After the bell rang, I lay in the ring bloodied and sore, a failure once again. My confidence was shaken, doubts about my ability to ever succeed in marriage surfaced, and fears of being forever alone plagued me. The desire for a special relationship was still there, but skepticism was creeping in. Would I be able to try again?

In subsequent years I worked in outpatient hemodialysis nursing, using medical equipment to remove impurities from the blood of patients who had kidney disease, and later transitioned into medical sales related to dialysis and cardiac care equipment and products. Training for hemodialysis nursing was intense, with in-depth study of the kidney and the many causes of kidney failure as well as hands-on practice with dialysis equipment simulating patient treatments. Practical application with patients did not begin until a good understanding of the equipment and potential problems that could occur during treatment was mastered. I worked with a team of professionals (physicians, dieticians, counselors) to provide care to an assigned group of chronic dialysis patients, as did the other registered nurses at the facility. The variety and complexity within the patient population was amazing, each person unique, with different diagnoses, physical abilities, social support systems, and qualities of life. What I saw on the surface was people trying to make the best of a bad situation that was out of their control. Some had hereditary kidney problems, some had suffered injuries, some had contributed to the kidney failure by the way they lived their lives. Some displayed anger; others avoided and refused to make changes; some accepted the condition and did everything possible to maintain life; for some hope was lost, and they gave up. When we received word of the unexpected death of one patient while he was on vacation, I sat on the floor of the nurses' station and wept quietly. This man had been a fighter, one who had not given up but was doing all he could to continue living as normal a life as possible. He was not ready to die. My weeping was about him and the loss of his life, but it was also about me. My life was a mess. I had failed at marriage twice, was continuing to fail at motherhood, and hated the monotony of my daily routine. My sadness over the patient's death mingled with my sadness over my own condition, and I felt ashamed. The patients I worked with faced daily challenges that I had never had to deal with, yet most of them fought to cling to life. How could I sit there on the floor feeling sorry for myself? This patient's life had value; it was precious. All life is precious no matter how difficult or messed up it may seem. Perhaps there was still hope in my heart.

During the years I worked in dialysis nursing my alcohol consumption continued to play a major role. Attending happy hour at local bars with a few female friends at the end of the work week was part of my routine. The low price of drinks and free food for a few hours seemed like such a good idea. When the special pricing ended, I had usually had more than enough to drink but continued to buy additional drinks at the regular price. Sometimes I connected with a man during the girls' night out, for drinks and too often for something more. As I look back over those years in my life, I am horrified at my risk-taking behavior. How desperate was I for attention, acceptance, and the hope for love that I would go off with a total stranger? Outrageous behavior, like swimming in apartment complex pools nude or standing up through the open sunroof of a moving vehicle, was not uncommon. Too often I left a bar late at night to drive home alone. My ability to drive was dangerously impaired, but by that time of night my ability to logically process the risk was gone. Sometimes, because of the effect of alcohol on my vision, I saw three lanes to drive in when there was only one. In the morning I would vow to not drive again after drinking heavily but the promise would fade away before my next bar adventure.

My use of alcohol and connections with some heavy drinkers during the later years of my dialysis nursing had a negative impact on my children. Following my divorce from Jim, I had been granted an overnight visitation every other weekend with my two sons. On one occasion, I awakened on a Saturday morning in a house where people had partied hard the night before. It was later than the time I was scheduled to pick up my children, and I was in no condition to pull myself together and go quickly to get them. I had to call and let them know I was not coming. Once again, I had let something get in the way of me being there for my sons. My focus on temporary pleasures, rather than their need for parental love, sent an unintended message to my sons: you do not matter as much to me as partying with my drinking buddies. I had made a choice; I put my alcohol consumption above my sons. It was the same message I had gotten when my dad spent time with his brothers drinking instead of with Mom and me. There is a generational cost related to addiction. My shame continued to mount as my abuse of alcohol pulled me down into a pit of despair. After the nights of heavy drinking I felt bad about myself. The nausea, vomiting, and headaches I experienced led me to vow to never again drink so much. I could refrain for a short time but would find something to celebrate with alcohol, fail to limit my intake, suffer the consequences of another hangover, and continue down the spiral into feelings of worthlessness. On one occasion, I got into a verbal fight at a bar and pool hall with the man who was living with me for a short time. He drove off with my car, and I was left to walk miles to my home. My mind was fuzzy as I started out, the result of an alcohol-induced blackout, and it took a while to get my bearings. Along the way a patrol car, with two police officers inside, stopped and asked for my ID. They were from a different jurisdiction from the area where I lived, so could not give me a ride. It was humiliating to be stopped that way, yet I counted myself fortunate that I did not end up in a drunk tank that night. Coworkers cautioned me about the people I was hanging out with and told me I was worth more than what I was accepting. My unspoken reply: you don't know how truly bad I am. By then I had pretty well written myself off, thinking I was of no value to myself or my children.

 The medical sales job that followed the years of nursing offered me many positives: air travel to various locations, learning product features, helping customers with product selection, training office staff, and providing ongoing support to them. I was fortunate to work with a good manager who understood the products well and the people he supervised even better. There were less-positive aspects of sales also: a high level of stress related to meeting annual quotas, inadequate time in any one place to develop friendships or intimate relationships, and easy access to alcohol and the resulting sexual encounters while traveling on business. A casual conversation with a man at the hotel bar or in a restaurant often led to numerous drinks, culminating in a physical encounter. Some men were single, others married, but it didn't matter to me. Sometimes I tried to rationalize that the alcohol was not a problem if I limited my drinking to weekends only. For a while I considered wine to be less of a problem and avoided drinking straight bourbon and martinis, which were two of my favorites. Other times I set limits on the number of drinks I would have during the evening. Too often I failed to live up to the self-imposed limit I had set and felt like a failure the following day. One time during a business trip, I awoke with a man in my bed, so fuzzy in my thinking that I could barely piece together details from the night before. Although I had not passed out, I could not recall portions of time from the night before. The black outs were occurring with greater frequency, and it seemed to take less alcohol for it to happen. It was unnerving!

The only conclusion I could come to was that there was no redeeming quality in me. My two marriages had failed. I had abandoned my children. My boys were safe with their dad. What did I really have to offer them? Yes, I was a good nurse, but somehow that didn't matter much when I considered my failures. I had little hope for myself.

## Chapter 3

## *Hope Dawning*

IT WAS DURING THE YEARS AS A MEDICAL SALES REPRE-sentative that I finally accepted the fact that alcohol was a serious problem for me. Even with the knowledge of addictions I had acquired as a nurse, I had still engaged in most of the typical coping behaviors: I tried to limit alcohol consumption to certain days of the week or month, to abstain from alcohol for certain periods of time, and to limit the amount or type of alcohol I consumed at each occasion. I knew from experience I was trying to fill some emptiness within me by drinking. My nurse's training had addressed the addiction cycle well, and I recognized that pattern in my efforts to control my own drinking. I had seen family members and friends struggle with addictions, but I had never understood how seemingly normal people could become so bogged down in alcohol or drugs. Now it was different; I was living with addiction myself. I was damaged goods. I could see how my feelings of guilt and shame escalated each time I failed to follow my own parameters. It was like stepping into quicksand and feeling it slowly suck me down. Each technique I used to control the addiction acted like a weight pulling me further down when it failed to work. Like the person trapped in quicksand, with arms flapping wildly about, my attempts only made things worse, pulling me down into the deadly muck. The dreams I recall from my drinking years seem to have a common theme: searching for and seeking something. Sometimes I dreamed I was attending school and looking for a classroom. Even if I had been to the class before, I was unable to find my way back to it. Other times I dreamed I was shopping and had seen something I liked. When I tried to return to the store to find the item again, either the item eluded me, or I could not locate the store. Feelings of anxiousness and despair accompanied the dreams. I was desperate to get to "something." There were also frightening dreams that involved snakes—poisonous snakes. I sometimes saw myself seated on a trapeze swinging in a jungle-like setting with deadly snakes below me. I felt panic as I clung to the ropes of the trapeze, trying not to fall from its safety onto the snakes below. That feeling of hanging on for safety, of not losing control, followed me into my waking hours. I diligently worked my sales territory, presented products, provided training on products to my customers, and was responsive to their calls and concerns. During the daytime I was focused on work where I had some sense of control over things. And yet, there were aspects of work beyond my control that hung over me much of the time: the fear of missing my sales quota; the fear of taking a drink during a business trip and not being able to stop; the fear of another black out and waking up somewhere unknown with a person I could not recall. Even in my waking hours, it felt like I was barely hanging on.

My medical equipment sales manager, Rich, had told me about Jesus Christ on more than one occasion during the years I worked with him. One winter day in 1986, after I resigned my position with the medical equipment company and after Rich completed the termination papers, he helped me load the U-Haul truck. He was driving the truck and me from Fremont, California to Phoenix, Arizona, where I would live with Roger in his home. When we reached Parker Dam, Rich pulled over and shared with me the story of salvation. He told me about God's love and the provision of His Son to pay the price for the sin of all mankind. I knew then that what he said was true. Somewhere deep inside me his words spoke truth. I knew that I was on a downward spiral, desperately lost and in need of Jesus, yet I turned away with tears streaming down my cheeks. I feared that my relationship with Roger (potentially husband number three) would end if I arrived at his home and said I needed to live my life differently. Our relationship, which began at a self-awareness workshop, included a sexual component from the beginning. At that point in my life, intimacy meant sex. It was not until years later that I realized the elusive thing I had been seeking much of my life was the intimacy of relationship, not the physical connection of sex or even the emotional approval of a loved one, but the spiritual intimacy available only in relationship with Christ. Moving in with a man and having a sexual relationship outside of marriage would not be right. Although I had not read the Bible, I knew there was a higher standard for living. I did not know then the risk I took by postponing the decision to accept Christ; however, in His mercy Christ did not give up on me or allow me to die before I believed in Him.

The apostle Paul, called Saul prior to his conversion experience, was zealous in his persecution of those who believed in Christ. During his encounter with Christ on the road to Damascus, Paul heard Christ speak clearly His purpose for Saul. "I will deliver you from the Jewish people, as well as from the Gentiles, to whom I now send you, to open their eyes, in order to turn them from darkness to light, and from the power of Satan to God, that they may receive forgiveness of sins and an inheritance among those who are sanctified by faith in Me," as written in the Book of Acts 26:17–18. Rich was faithful to continue telling me about salvation in Christ even though I stopped working in medical sales for a while. Each time he did, I felt uncomfortable, not aware that I was experiencing conviction of the need to have a personal relationship with Christ. I could, however, see how this man related to his wife and daughter, as well as recall how he treated his sales representatives and worked with upper management. Philippians 2:14–15 says, "Do all things without complaining and disputing, that you may become blameless and harmless, children of God without fault in the midst of a crooked and perverse generation, among whom you shine as lights in the world." There was something different about Rich that continued to draw me to the source of his character and allowed me to hear his message of salvation. My fear of losing Roger kept me from acting on it.

One thing I avoided after my second divorce was a rebound marriage; it was not until December 1987, five years later, that I married for the third time. The old idea that the "right person" would make the difference still lingered in my mind, however, and I left myself open to unmet expectations once again. Nearly a year later, I enrolled in a MBA program at a local university. My manager at a local health maintenance organization (HMO) had suggested my nursing degree would not be taken as seriously as a business degree if I hoped for advancement in the HMO. Higher education also fit into my self-improvement plan for fixing my life. If I could acquire more education and have a better paying job and a happy marriage, then everything would be okay, and I would finally be happy. The first two years of my third marriage were rough. Each of us had exhibited our best behavior while dating, and once the veil was pulled back, I was not so sure I liked what I saw in my new spouse or myself. I did not give up, however, not wanting to be a failure once again, not wanting to be a "three-time loser" at the marriage game. In 1990, my drinking problem turned out to be the blessing that saved our marriage.

My celebration of a girlfriend's birthday one night turned into a heavy-drinking affair when the short-staffing at the restaurant resulted in us having permission to refill our wine glasses. The refills were frequent, and I became flirtatious with some of the male diners, even inviting one to come back to my house to play a board game. My girlfriend escorted me home, where I made a lot of noise saying goodnight to her in the foyer. My husband was already in bed and gave no indication of being awake, although he later said that he heard me and considered my behavior inconsiderate. In the morning I went to the master bathroom and sat on the toilet, wondering where I had left my clothes the night before. Too many times in the past I had awakened not knowing where I had left clothing, exactly what I had done the night before, and resolving not to drink so much again. This time I was horrified as I recalled what had nearly happened the night before. As I sat there, I cried out, "God, help me! I can't do this anymore!" My games with alcohol, my controlling of events, my rationalizations, my guilt, and my shame, all had reached a climax. The date was February 11, 1990. I had finally reached the end of myself. My eyes were finally opened. I had turned from darkness to light, from the power of Satan to God.

Rich and his wife invited us to their church on Easter Sunday that year, and I read the words of salvation on a brochure and formally accepted Jesus Christ. Those who knew me best knew that something significant had already happened when I cried out to God in the privacy of my own bathroom. That was the moment I surrendered my will to Jesus and gave Him control of my life. The change in me and my behavior was immediate. What transpired on Easter Sunday was the outward manifestation of the change that had already occurred within me when I cried out to God on February 11, 1990. The words of 1 John 5:4 say, "For whatever is born of God overcomes the world. And this

*Finding Hope*

is the victory that has overcome the world—our faith." By my faith in Jesus, I had become an overcomer. The temptation of alcohol and the lure of illicit sex had lost their power over me. The words of Christ in John 16:33 say, "These things I have spoken to you, that in Me you may have peace. In the world you will have tribulation; but be of good cheer, I have overcome the world." My efforts at self-control were futile. Only by recognizing the light I saw in a friend and responding to the truth he spoke have I found the peace of Christ.

## Chapter 4

# Power To Change

After my public acceptance of Christ, on Easter morning 1990, Roger and I joined Rich and his family at a local resort for an elaborate Easter brunch. My memories of the day are rich and warm: strolling along a path with Eddie, Rich's wife, on the way to the brunch; beautiful flowers blooming beneath a bright blue Arizona sky; feeling like a princess in the ivory two-piece dress I wore, with its soft pleated skirt and decorative pocket trim; enjoying the sense of being part of a family as we conversed during the meal; having Rich refer to me as "little sister" as we talked about my new birth in Christ. Rich acted as a mentor gifting me with a study Bible and helping us connect with a local Bible teaching church. Initially I felt uncomfortable going to church, that hovering sense of inadequacy, of not being good enough to attend, rearing its ugly head. I gripped Roger's hand tightly as we walked into church the first time. There were so many people streaming between the parking lot and church as they navigated the multiple service sessions on Sunday mornings. I observed the fancy dress of many of the people attending, and it seemed they were so much more put together than I was. Everything was new to me: the way the music, the pastor's message, and the participation by attendees came together; finding my way in the Bible that was still new to me, referencing scripture as the pastor taught; receiving the communion bread and cup for the first time. It was not long before I learned the feelings of inadequacy were not unique to me alone, and they did not keep me from returning to church week after week.

I found I did not have to achieve some level of perfection before I was worthy of attending church. I had acknowledged my sin to God, repented of it, and asked for forgiveness. I was forgiven, just as others in the church who had done the same. When Jesus died on the cross, He took the sin of the world upon Himself, paying the price for all mankind, and providing the way for me to have a personal relationship with God. As Jesus celebrated the Passover meal with His disciples prior to His death, He spoke the words recorded in John 14:16–17: "And I will pray the Father, and He will give you another Helper, that He may abide with you forever—the Spirit of truth, whom the world cannot receive, because it neither sees Him nor knows Him; but you know Him, for He dwells with you and will be in you." God's power was available, with the Holy Spirit dwelling in me, to help me change and become more like His Son, Jesus Christ. Armed with that knowledge, I began daily Bible reading and joined a women's Bible study. I was hungry to read God's word, to pray both alone and with other women, and to develop Christlikeness. The awkwardness I felt the first time I prayed aloud with a small group of women soon faded away, replaced by a sense of acceptance and belonging. There was a sense of being part of a family that cares for every member, no matter what has occurred previously with them or is happening now, and will be faithful to support one another through the difficult times.

God delivered me from bondage to alcohol when I cried out to Him on February 11, 1990. God's word in Romans 8:28 states, "And we know that all things work together for good to those who love God, to those who are the called according to His purpose." When I yield to Jesus, my deliverer, and remain obedient to refrain from alcohol, I am freed from this sin. First Corinthians 10:13 says, "No temptation has overtaken you except such as is common to man; but God is faithful, who will not allow you to be tempted beyond what you are able, but with the temptation will also make the way of escape, that you may be able to bear it." In the ensuing years there have been times of temptation, not frequently and usually connected with a trial of some kind, but God has always provided a way of escape or given me the strength to bear it. Taking my fears of temptation to God, crying out to Jesus in prayer, asking for strength and guidance, has been my way of escape. I have found that being in His word, actively seeking scripture that applies to my situation and incorporating it into my prayers has been my greatest source of strength. When I bow before the Lord, sincerely confessing my need and acknowledging His great power, temptation fades away, and a feeling of safety returns.

I consider my deliverance from alcohol to be a gift from God, one that I hold dear. When my older son was married in 2015, I attended the wedding, held in an all-inclusive resort environment in the Caribbean. I knew alcohol would be freely available throughout my stay and there would be celebratory toasts at the wedding reception. Prayer prior to my trip and throughout it was powerful: "Mighty God, You have freed me from the grip of alcohol in my life. It is not by my power, strength, or any other ability that I have been released from bondage to alcohol. It is You, with Your loving hand of restraint, keeping me safe from alcohol. Keep me during my journey from becoming complacent, from taking for granted the freedom I now experience. For if I become overly confident in any area of my life, failing to see that it is You in control, not me, then I risk succumbing to pride. The sobriety You have provided for so many years could be lost in an instant if I take my eyes off you, Lord Jesus. Thank you for protecting and keeping me throughout this wonderful event." My prayer was answered. My ability to enjoy the tropical setting, the group dinners, and my solitary time was neither impacted nor diminished in any way by my refraining from alcohol. On my son's wedding day, my water glass was raised high to toast the bride and groom as I shared heartfelt words with both of them and the guests gathered at the table.

In 2001, Roger and I decided to move from Arizona to Oregon. However, he agreed to stay with his employer through the closure of one Arizona plant and was living in an apartment there until his assignment was completed, while I completed the move ahead of him. One of my first priorities after settling into our Oregon home in 2001 was to connect with a Bible teaching church. It was through my connection with a local church that I learned of a small group opportunity. In 2002 I participated in a small group Bible study in Roseburg, Oregon, based on material from the Biblical Counseling Foundation. The intense reading and application of scripture between group sessions resulted in tremendous spiritual growth for me. Jesus's words in John 16:8 say, "And when He has come, He will convict the world of sin, and of righteousness, and of judgment." Through the power of the Holy Spirit, by His conviction, I saw my personal sin that was impacting and hindering our marriage. My critical spirit and lack of forgiveness toward my husband had resulted in bitterness and resentment that would destroy our marriage if left unchecked. I had fallen into a habit of comparing myself to my husband in the area of spiritual growth and seeing myself as more advanced than him.

My husband made a profession of faith in Jesus on Easter Sunday in 1990, as I had. He had seen the change in me since I cried out to God on February 11, 1990. My conversion experience had been dramatic, and observable change was immediate. His conversion experience was intentional but not dramatic, his relationship with Jesus developing gradually as he faithfully read scripture. Our expressions of praise and worship were different, and the way we responded to scripture and interacted with people was different, so I began to question my husband's spirituality. I wrote notes in my devotion books and in the Bible, especially when there were messages or scripture related to how believers are to live. If I had experienced hurt or disappointment with my husband in one of these areas, I saw the spiritual teaching as something he needed. All the while I ignored the scriptures and devotions that spoke of my critical, judgmental attitude toward my husband regarding his personal relationship with the Lord. I read some of the devotion books yearly, and each time I saw an earlier notation, it brought up a past hurt and opened a wound that was still festering. Obviously, I had not forgiven a perceived offense or hurt, and it was my disobedience that was driving a wedge between me and my husband. In his *Experiencing God* devotional book, Henry Blackaby speaks of the way we are changed by meditation on God's word. He says, "You cannot have Scripture fill your heart and continue to sin against God. When God's truth is allowed to touch the deepest corner of your soul, the Holy Spirit will transform you into the image of Jesus Christ."[1] As the psalmist said in Psalm 119:11, "Your word I have hidden in my heart, that I might not sin against You." God convicted me during this Bible study of my sin, filled me with the desire to obey His word, and changed my heart and attitude toward my husband.

---

[1] Henry T. & Richard Blackaby, *Experiencing God Day By Day, Devotional* (Nashville, TN: B&H Publishing Group, 2006) 102.

It is easy in marriage to recognize failures, weaknesses, and flaws in our mates; however, it is often much more difficult to see our own issues. It is easy to recognize something is not quite right yet justify our own behavior and avoid calling it what it truly is, sin. One of the key scriptures that helped me during the study was Matthew 7:1–5: "Judge not, that you be not judged. For with what judgment you judge, you will be judged; and with the measure you use, it will be measured back to you. And why do you look at the speck in your brother's eye, but do not consider the plank in your own eye? Or how can you say to your brother, 'Let me remove the speck from your eye'; and look, a plank is in your own eye? Hypocrite! First remove the plank from your own eye, and then you will see clearly to remove the speck from your brother's eye." Another scripture, Ephesians 4:31–32, provided specific direction regarding behaviors that had become entrenched in me over the years. "Let all bitterness, wrath, anger, clamor, and evil speaking be put away from you, with all malice. And be kind to one another, tenderhearted, forgiving one another, even as God in Christ forgave you." When I looked at my own behavior, it seemed my greatest sin was lack of forgiveness. The critical spirit, resentment, and bitterness all flowed from my failure to forgive. When I am tempted to simmer over something my husband has done or not done that I wanted him to do, or for some words he spoke or failed to speak, I now come under the conviction of the Holy Spirit. Is there anything my spouse could say or do that is more hurtful or unaware than the way I treated Christ for so long? I was not good, kind, loving, or tenderhearted and yet Christ forgave me. Whenever I feel stubbornness, bitterness, or resentment kicking in, I remember Christ's forgiveness of me and in obedience to Him, I choose to forgive. The unconditional love I have for my husband is only possible because of the changed heart God has given me. "He has delivered us from the power of darkness and conveyed us into the kingdom of the Son of His love, in whom we have redemption through His blood, the forgiveness of sins" (Col. 1:14–15). God changes lives: overcoming addictions, providing escape from temptation, convicting of personal sin, changing hearts, and delivering from the power of darkness. The power to change comes from my relationship with Christ.

## Chapter 5

# Relationships Matter

THERE IS A PATTERN OF REPETITION IN MY JOURNAL entries over the years since I placed my faith in Christ: feelings of grief and sadness when things are amiss in my relationships with others, resulting in me desperately seeking Him. Prior to accepting Christ, my primary focus was on accomplishments, possessions, being accepted by others, and finding happiness. My focus was on myself, not others, and their well-being was not a high priority in my decision-making process. Relationships existed, some supportive and pleasant, others not so positive and somewhat draining in nature, but I did not value highly the relationship itself. Whenever there was disagreement within the relationship over an issue, my standard ways of reconciling differences were compromise or giving in. Sometimes I stubbornly dug in on my own position, refusing to hear what the other person had to say, and refused to budge. The result was a lot of unresolved baggage, unmet expectations, hurt feelings, and damaged relationships.

One of the things I learned as I matured in my faith was the importance of placing God on the throne of my life, not self. During a sermon one pastor described it as having a capital "S," representing the Spirit of God, in control of our lives rather than a small "s," self, in charge. That picture, providing a changed perspective, made a great difference in how I began to live my life. My primary relationship now is with God, the One who is on the throne of my life. All other relationships are secondary to that one, with my next highest priority being the relationship with my husband, followed by my children, close friends and family, and other significant contacts. Every relationship is influenced by my relationship with God. When my relationship with Him is not right, there is a trickle-down effect on all the others. If I stay focused on

God and view every situation, every relationship, from His perspective, things go much better in my communications with others.

My relationship with my husband has changed over the years, becoming stronger as we have both grown in our faith. God allows us to see each other through His eyes when we listen to His word and are obedient to it. We have learned to communicate in love things that matter to us: hurts we feel, different viewpoints, our fears, hopes, and frustrations. We are not perfect people, and we still reach impasses on occasion. The difference is that we now look out for each other's well-being, not valuing things more highly than our relationship, and we have learned to appreciate each other even when we are not in agreement. We can do that only when we allow the Spirit of God to control of our lives.

In our early years together, prior to my accepting Jesus, Roger's mom washed one of my summer outfits and dried it on a high temperature setting. It was a favorite outfit I wore during my sales visits to some of the rural areas of Arizona. It was comfortable, business-casual in style, and travelled well in my suitcase when I was driving for several days to see customers. When I started to put it on the first time after her washing, it didn't fit; it was shriveled up and looked comical on me. The top and skirt had both shrunk —severely; the outfit was useless to me. I was furious! I could not undo the damage done, and I wanted revenge. Roger's mom was in the process of buying the house he had owned with his first wife, and Mom was living in it with us while our new home was being built in a different area of town. There were three of us in the small home, and there was no way for me to escape the long-term tension between the two of them. On one prior occasion his mom had yelled at both of us and called me his whore; he had remained silent, with no response. When I first moved into the home, pictures of his first wife, one of her in her wedding dress, still hung on the wall. It was a constant reminder of that relationship and made we wonder what ties remained between them. How secure was his new relationship with me? My fear of rejection, of taking second place to his ex-wife, his mother, or his two small dogs was growing. Although he had nothing to do with the damage to my outfit, I was angry with him more than with his mother. I had expected him to stand up for me against his mother, to somehow put her in her place for damaging my outfit, to show support for me. I had wanted him to stand up to his mother previously when she called me his whore. Was that all I really was to him? And I had wanted him to be so sensitive to my feelings and the impact the ex-wife's pictures on the wall would have on me that he would take them down without me having to say anything to him. On this occasion the cumulative unmet expectations erupted into anger that spoke so loudly that he could not sense what was in my heart. I never gave him a chance to help me. I failed to communicate to him the support I wanted and needed from him. When he didn't meet my unspoken needs, I felt rejected and turned inward with my accumulating fears. Could I be resigned to a lifetime of this? Wasn't there something better in store for us? I let a ruined summer outfit, a simple thing, trigger my angry feelings and take on greater value than maintaining a healthy relationship with my fiancé.

One event during the early years of our marriage was traumatic, and it took years for me to recover fully. It was, in fact, one of the recollections that helped me to realize just how important the relationship itself is. One day as I was dusting and polishing furniture in our new home, a small portion broke off a piece of artwork, the beak of a porcelain bird in flight. I wasn't even aware it had happened until Roger noticed the beak was missing when he came home from work that afternoon. The bird was a sandpiper just taking flight, one of several in the piece he had acquired prior to meeting me. It was a beautiful, fragile selection of art that had significance to him beyond its looks. He was devastated by what he saw and angry at me. We searched the area repeatedly for the beak with no success. I felt terrible about the damage I had done and worse when we could not find the beak; it seemed all hope of repair was gone. There was stony silence between us for days that no amount of apology on my part could change. I thought our relationship was damaged irrevocably and experienced tears flowing freely during that time. Things improved somewhat once he located a person in our area who was skilled in the restoration of art pieces. Conversation began to return in our home as hope rose in both of us that the piece could be restored, the damage repaired. He picked up the artwork to carry it to the garage for protective wrapping prior to transport and, in the process, the bird separated from the base portion. The pieces did not drop to the floor and shatter, thank goodness, but the restoration job had gotten bigger. My husband was able to chuckle later about his near-miss with disaster and voiced the relief he felt knowing that both mishaps could be repaired.

Twenty years later I had a similar experience with another piece of artwork, also purchased prior to us meeting, and the lingering memory of the first incident hung like a dark cloud over me. One night while I was ironing in our living room, the ironing board tipped a bit, and the iron toppled toward the floor. I desperately tried to grab the power cord as the hot iron fell to keep it from crashing onto the tile floor below. The tile was unscathed but the art piece, a soapstone family of elephants positioned on the tile near the ironing board, was damaged. The surface was chipped in several places from the iron bouncing off it onto the padded carpet nearby. I was horrified as I realized there was no way I would be able to fix the damage done. I dreaded telling my husband, fearing a repeat of the bird event from years earlier. For months I kept the leaves of an adjacent silk plant arranged in such a way that the damage to the elephants was less noticeable. Eventually I confessed what had happened and how I feared it damaging our relationship. This time he responded differently, calmly reassuring me the damage could be repaired. Our relationship was what mattered to him, more than the piece of artwork. The days of tears and anguish over a broken art object are behind us, and we are finally able to laugh at some of the things we experienced in our early years together.

I find satisfaction in a job well done but can accept less than perfection in many outcomes, and I tend to look at the big picture. Over the years, we have learned to complement each other rather than resist as we did in our early years, and our relationship has benefited from the change. Now when we shop and see two options for a project, instead of deliberating long and leaving the store empty-handed because we couldn't reach a decision, we purchase both options and return the one we end up not using. When the vision I have for decorating a room falls apart and I am in despair because the textures, colors, or materials I chose are not working well, he helps me regroup and modify the plan. My husband is able to listen and hear my heart about what I hope to accomplish rather than simply telling me what I need to do; then he helps me find another way to accomplish it. I have learned to adjust my pace when we work together on a project, slowing down so

I can appreciate the satisfaction he takes in his completed work rather than becoming impatient at the amount of time it is taking. What we have experienced goes beyond a change in communication style. It is a change of heart that has made the difference in our relationship. I treasure the words of Philippians 2:3–4 which say, "Let nothing be done through selfish ambition or conceit, but in lowliness of mind let each esteem others better than himself. Let each of you look out not only for his own interests, but also for the interest of others." In Matthew 11:29, the Lord Jesus referred to Himself as, "gentle and lowly in heart." My relationship with my husband works best when we, too, have lowliness of mind, consider each other and are willing to adjust our plans accordingly.

My relationship with my dad changed as I began to see him through God's eyes, becoming precious in the years between February 1990 and his death in October 1996. Prior to that, there was frequent tension between us, often regarding his use of alcohol, even though I drank alcohol on a regular basis. When he visited Arizona during the early years of my first marriage, I tried to control his drinking, without success, and felt frustration rather than enjoyment over the time I had with him in my home. One day he disappeared for hours, returning later to tell me about the nice people he had spent time with at a little hole-in-the-wall neighborhood bar. I was angry. I was hurt. My mom had just died, and I had hoped Dad's visit to the apartment where Jim and I lived would be a time of healing and remembering for both of us. Yet, he had found relief in the hours he spent in the company of strangers, at a smoke-filled bar overlooking an indoor ice-skating rink. I had not even been included. In my desire for connection with my dad I tried to "fix" him. My focus was on his alcohol consumption, the supposed culprit, rather than looking into the many facets that make up a good relationship. I could not accept my dad and love him as he was and only drove a greater wedge between us with my long-distance efforts to control his behavior. What we had was a power struggle, far from a healthy relationship.

Once I acknowledged my own alcoholism nearly twenty years later, my perspective toward my dad changed. How could I be so judgmental and controlling when I struggled with the same issue? Even before I accepted Christ, I began to feel concern for him rather than being angry and attempting to change him. As I became aware of the frequency of his drinking and the amount of his alcohol consumption, I was frightened about his health and the potential for people to take advantage of him financially. Our primary connection was through phone calls, with letters, notes, and a few trips to see each other in person over the years. Dad enjoyed sharing pictures with me of the progress he was making on the home he was building in Bandon, Oregon, and I took pleasure in seeing his dream coming true. He was finally in a location where trees, streams, and the ocean all came together, a place where he could enjoy fishing and hunting and live in a home created with his own hands. It was during this time that our long-distance relationship began to grow.

During my second employment in medical sales, I had an opportunity to go see my dad one weekend, fitting the visit between the days I was working with the Portland-based sales representative. During that brief visit I saw how drastically my dad's health had deteriorated. He was having significant memory issues and was extremely thin. There had been concern at his local bank that he might not be managing his money well and was vulnerable to financial abuse by people in the community. It was obvious to me that he needed more support than I could provide long distance. The big question was, would Dad be willing to move to Arizona where he could be near me? My dad had been the biggest authority figure in my life for years, and the idea of asking him to give up his independence, to leave his dream area, seemed almost impossible. I expected a tremendous fight as I gathered courage to make the phone call to ask him to move to Arizona. The dread I felt as I dialed was quickly replaced by complete surprise at his response; Dad was relieved at the offer of help but had not wanted to be a bother, so he had not asked for help. Dad was soon able to move into a little ground floor efficiency apartment in an independent living facility located about fifteen minutes from the home where Roger and I lived. Although Dad had not been able to complete his dream home on the Oregon coast, his move allowed us to experience closeness in our relationship that we had never known before.

During the nearly five years Dad lived in independent living we saw each other weekly, more often once I stopped working in medical sales. We enjoyed visits to the Phoenix Zoo, taking walks and short hikes, and going out for breakfast or dinner at favorite restaurants. Feeding the pigeons while we took breaks in the zoo snack area and watching the cheetahs chase raw meat attached to a wire that was pulled rapidly through their zoo enclosure were great treats for both of us. Breakfast at Denny's and dinner at a local Mexican restaurant were among his favorites. When Denny's ran a special on mugs at Christmas one year, Dad insisted on getting me the Rudolph mug. When a hot beverage was poured into the mug, Rudolph's nose would light up, the white of his nose taking on a rosy tone as the cup was filled. I still have that cup and smile when I recall the pleasure Dad had in giving it to me.

During our visits we reminisced about people and places from the past, especially as his memory declined and the long-term memories were clearest for him. Throughout Dad's time in independent living, he was able to go on weekly shopping trips with other residents, and he continued to buy alcohol. By this point in his life, wine had become his favorite drink. As God continued to change my heart, I realized my dad was no more flawed than me, no more a sinner than me, and that his intentions had been good toward me and my mom. Dad's focus during my childhood was on providing financially for his family. He thought that by doing that, he was being a good husband and father. He grew up thinking boys don't cry, and showing emotion is not right for men. The result was a man who had good motives, a right heart, but no sense of the importance of relationship, including the power of a kind word or touch and time spent focused on a loved one. My earthly father was with me only a short time, as God views time, yet there are so many good memories of our time together.

On my dad's seventy-fifth birthday, I presented him with a framed tribute that he hung proudly in his little efficiency apartment. The idea came from the book *The Tribute*, by Dennis Rainey with David Boehi, discovered at a Family Life conference Roger and I attended in Arizona. After reading the book, I was able to take memories and qualities conveyed to me by my dad and present them to him in a way that honored him. I am thankful that God allowed me to love my dad and appreciate him so much in his final years. I was able to see him through God's eyes as I grew in my Christian walk. Luke 11:11–13 speaks so clearly of the concern earthly fathers have for their children. Verse 13 says, "If you then, being evil, know how to give good gifts to your children, how much more will your heavenly Father give the Holy

Spirit to those who ask Him!" I do not know if my dad ever accepted Jesus as his Savior. I do know that he surprised me one year by singing, in a beautiful, clear voice, words to Christmas hymns during an event at the church we attended. He was not looking at words in print; they were simply coming from some memory deep within. It touched me and brought a glimmer of hope; perhaps there had been some church attendance many years ago, some seeds of faith planted. I could only pray that he would listen when I shared the gospel story and respond; one day I will know.

My sense of regret regarding relationships is greatest when I think of my two sons. So many precious opportunities were lost over the years due to the way I lived my life prior to accepting Christ in 1990. There was no mom to welcome them home at the end of the school day, to transport them to and from school events, to encourage them daily, and to show them a mother's love. As I consider the things that were lost, I see the past through my current perspective. I see positive experiences my sons would have experienced if I had been living my life in the way I now do. The losses I see are based on my Christian perspective. That was not the case, however, and the mother and role model they experienced in me during childhood was not positive. What would the cost have been to my sons if I had remained with them but not changed how I lived my life?

One conversation with my older son reminded me of just how coarse I could be with my comments and how unkind I could be. I did not remember the driving incident, with me cursing and yelling at another driver, but he did, and the fact that such a dismal incident was one that remains clear to him after so many years made me cringe. I am not proud of my past behavior and was grieved that this was what my son recalled. What kind of monster was I? I turned to God in prayer, filled with remorse: "Oh, Lord, You know my heart. You know all things. You know my failings as a mom; my regrets over being such a poor role model to my sons. Though I failed miserably, You never stopped loving me. You have not left me in my sins and trespasses, nor have You forsaken me in my weakness. Thank you, Lord, for restoring my soul."

Over the years, God has shown me the great value of the relationships I have with my sons. Children are good gifts from the Lord, precious gifts that He entrusts to parents for a time. Because my focus was on self, not God, during my sons' childhoods, I was not able to show them the love and care they deserved. The parable in the Bible of the lost son, Luke 15:11–32, feels personal because of a period of estrangement between me and my older son. During the time of separation, I never stopped praying for reconciliation, for the restoration of our relationship. As I look back on the situation, it is easier to see how my firm stand on a topic came between us. As a reasonably new Christian, I desired the best for my sons and hoped they could avoid some of the poor choices I had made. I also did not want to condone behaviors in my sons that I knew were not right in God's eyes. It must have been difficult for my son to hear me set limits on him that I had never set for myself. Hypocrite! I am sure it seemed like a double standard and must have felt like I was rejecting him for not living up to my new standards. In any event, we had infrequent, strained communications for several years. I had written to both of my sons in 1995 asking forgiveness for the way I had hurt them by the way I lived my life. A year later I wrote to my older son asking forgiveness for my judgmental attitude. The day he called, ready for renewal of our relationship, was a day of great celebration. He later shared that a girlfriend and his dad had encouraged him to reconnect with me. Many coworkers and volunteers at the Crisis Pregnancy Center where I worked at the time knew of the estrangement between me and my son; they prayed faithfully that it would be restored. The words of James 5:16 say, "The effective, fervent prayer of a righteous man avails much." My sons have become strong, capable men despite my failings as a parent. Both seem uncomfortable when I speak of not having been a good mom and tell me that I was "a good mom." Perhaps their perspective also has been influenced by the way I now live my life.

My younger son, now divorced, once spoke with me about circumstances regarding his failed marriage. He has come to realize that I was supportive of his wife as well as them as a couple, and he appreciated it. My older son seemed unlikely for years to marry, citing my two divorces and his friends' divorces, yet he made the commitment in 2015. Each time he discussed marriage with me I told him I believed the only way marriages can succeed is by having God at the head of the union. One of my gifts for their wedding was a framed guideline for a happy marriage, sharing God's word that has been so important for me in my third marriage. The words of Isaiah 55:11 inspired me to create this gift for my son and his bride: "So shall My word be that goes forth from My mouth; It shall not return to Me void, But it shall accomplish what I please, And it shall prosper in the thing for which I sent it." My older son once commented that he had never seen me waver in my faith. My sons have seen the differences in my marriages and the impact my personal relationship with Christ has made.

Relationships matter: they require time, attention, self-denial, love and forgiveness to succeed and flourish. When my relationship with God is not right, there is a trickle-down effect on all the other relationships in my life. A right relationship with Christ is the key to success in relationships.

## Chapter 6

# *Overcoming Trials*

THE TRIALS IN MY LIFE HAVE BEEN A TRAINING FIELD, the place where I have come to know Christ better. His character and qualities have been revealed during some of the darkest, most difficult times: health issues, death, job challenges, and disputes. During those times I sought God often, crying out to Him in prayer, thanking Him for being there, for guiding me, for answering in His way and in His timing. I never felt completely alone or without hope when I stayed near Him. While enduring trials I saw blessings and made a point of writing in a journal so I could later recall the important lessons learned. Perhaps the greatest lesson learned is the faithfulness of God, a quality extolled many times by David in the Old Testament Psalms. In Psalm 36:5 he says, "Your mercy, O LORD, is in the heavens; Your faithfulness reaches to the clouds." In Psalm 40:10, David tells how he has responded to God: "I have declared Your faithfulness and Your salvation." The words of Psalm 89:1–2 further proclaim David's confidence in God: "I will sing of the mercies of the LORD forever; with my mouth will I make known Your faithfulness to all generations. Your faithfulness You shall establish in the very heavens." And in Psalm 143, a psalm of lament, David cries out in verse 1: "Hear my prayer, O LORD, give ear to my supplications! In Your faithfulness answer me, and in Your righteousness." I followed David's example and cried out to God during the personal trials in my own life.

The lament psalms of the Old Testament are filled with the emotional words of a suffering person. There is simplicity in the approach to God, with the petitioner sometimes beginning by merely calling out His name in distress, nothing more. The suffering person pours out his situation to God, sometimes accusing God of not caring. There are feelings of being forsaken and helpless resulting from this wrong assumption. Often, it seems there is an enemy winning the battle, spiritual or physical, and the sufferer has no hope. There is a confession of trust in God, against all odds, and a plea for deliverance from the trial the person is going through. The lament psalms conclude with a promise that the writer will praise God. Feelings of anguish, grief, and despair often lead me to cry out as the psalmists did. Sometimes I am speechless, not knowing what to say, how to begin; at those times, I simply cry out, "Oh, God! Help me!" God hears me. When the hopelessness of my situation is overwhelming, only God can ease my pain. Somewhere in the middle of my crying out to Him, spilling out the details, I realize God will never leave me or forsake me. When I recall the words of Joshua 31:6, "He will not leave you nor forsake you," there is no doubt that God cares for me. I, like the psalmists, acknowledge my trust in Him and the certainty that my hope is in Him. In my lamentation the burden eases, and I find my hope renewed. The lament psalms are a beautiful example, showing me how I need to respond during times of suffering.

My dad's declining health and eventually his death, a trial spanning a period of five-and-a-half years, was my first experience going through something difficult as a Christian. Dad's final year was the most intense time, with his rapidly declining health and ever-changing needs for care resulting in frequent adjustments to plans previously made. During our treasured, frequent visits to the Phoenix Zoo, Dad began referring to zebras as horses with stripes; he forgot how to tell time, and he could not remember me putting a miniature Christmas tree in his efficiency apartment a few days earlier. The memory issues I had hoped were simply part of the normal aging process had intensified to the point where I sought additional medical evaluation for Dad. A neurological exam early in 1996 resulted in a diagnosis of alcohol dementia, possibly Alzheimer disease, something that could only be confirmed by autopsy. It was obvious the days of him being able to live independently were coming to an end, and I would need to find another living arrangement for him. One of the blessings I experienced then came in the form of a friend from my women's Bible study group. As a social worker at a local hospital, she was familiar with assisted living and foster home options in the area, and she was able to provide me with direction on how to

*Finding Hope*

begin the search. I worked with the administration at Dad's independent living center to ensure paperwork was signed by Dad that would allow me to make decisions for him when he was no longer mentally or physically able to do so himself. I relied on God for the words to speak with my dad, wanting him to hear my concern for him and not reject my efforts to help. Dad was already exhibiting paranoid thinking about his money, and I feared he would refuse to sign the necessary paperwork. He did sign under the supervision of the administrator for the independent living facility, and I moved ahead with the search for an assisted living facility that would be a good fit for my dad.

In addition to the challenge facing me with Dad, Roger left soon afterward for South Korea on a seven-month assignment for his employer, so I was left alone to explore the options and make decisions for my dad's care. In his final year Dad had a medical emergency, a ruptured appendix, and was admitted to the hospital adjacent to his independent living facility. He was there for a month, until mid-March, and I spent many hours in the hospital chapel praying during his one-month stay. During the first few days I asked God to bring him through surgery, to make his pain bearable, and to restore his mind when he hallucinated. The women in my Bible study group knew about my dad's hospitalization and were all praying for both of us. Though I was alone, with my husband in distant Seoul, I was never truly alone. I saw God's hand in many ways on the day my car broke down on the way to visit Dad: a woman I knew from my earlier sales job stopped to offer help; a stranger let me into her home to use her phone so I could call for roadside assistance; AAA sent two tow trucks, not the standard one, in response to my service call; a friend responded immediately to my call for help and provided rides to the hospital and car dealer. During that phase of the trial I wrote in my journal: "I feel closer to God than I ever have before. Maybe it's good that I seem to be 'experiencing God' more during the trials." The Bible study I was attending at that time was *Experiencing God* by Henry Blackaby and Claude King. God's supernatural protection was the only explanation I had for the way the pieces came together that day when so much seemed to be falling apart. I was not alone that day; a loving God who knew my every need was my provider that day.

My husband returned home for a brief visit just before Dad's discharge from the hospital on March 11. For weeks I had been checking out placement options that would meet the needs of a person with the combined physical and memory issues my dad had. One company operated several group homes for people with dementia, providing twenty-four-hour care in a homelike setting, and seemed like a good option since one of their homes was just a short drive from my home. Residents shared bedrooms, had access to all living areas in the large home, and received nutritious meals and snacks daily. The setting was not pretentious and seemed like something Dad could enjoy if his strength returned sufficiently to allow him to spend time in the secured back yard. Dad was at the group home for only six days before taking a bad fall, related to low blood pressure, and he spent the next five weeks in the hospital. During those weeks I feared Dad was about to die, and I again spent hours in the hospital chapel on my knees in prayer. The chapel was always deserted when I sought refuge there at night, and I felt God's hand over me, His presence, and His comfort with me as I knelt and cried out to Him. Tears would stream down my face as I talked to God, with hot tears and tender knees, but eventually I would feel a sense of calm come over me, and I would be able to drive home and sleep in peace. Psalm 55:22 says, "Cast your burden on the LORD, and He shall sustain you; He shall never permit the righteous to be moved." In the act of pouring out my heart to God and crying out for strength and wisdom as the psalmists did, my burden transferred from me to my Lord. It was as if a heavy load slipped easily from my shoulders onto His. With that burden eased, I could put my head on the pillow and trust that everything was safe and secure with the Lord while I slept.

During one visit near the end of Dad's first week in the hospital, he did not know me. His words made it clear he thought I was my mom at a time in their life many years earlier. My anguish at Dad's rapid mental decline was eased by a phone call from my social worker friend. Just when I was at my low point with discouragement rearing its ugly head, she called, offering a listening ear and words of encouragement. God's timing is always perfect, even if it is not the timing we want. In early April, I agreed to have a feeding tube surgically placed in my dad to improve his nutrition. There was some possibility the dementia was related to the poor nutrition that was part of his alcoholism, and this minimally invasive procedure was something I could not ignore. Dad had always talked matter-of-factly about death, saying he did not want any heroic measures taken when his time came. I wanted to honor his wishes but not miss some basic medical intervention that might improve his health. I also knew Dad would not want to live "like a vegetable," based on past conversations with him. Although a feeding tube was not considered a heroic life-saving measure in health care, it might prolong his years of dementia. Was that something he would want? The decision was not something I easily reached.

During the latter part of April, Dad was transferred to a long-term care unit at the hospital as a hospice patient. The discharge planners looked ahead to potential dates for his transfer out of the facility, and I resumed, in earnest, my search for a care setting that would meet his increased level of need. I felt the pressure, like balancing on a wire high above the circus ring, to find safe care and still manage his remaining finances wisely. I worried about how long the funds would have to last, despaired over some of the facilities I visited, and continued talking to God about all of it. While I was at the Department of Health Services checking complaint histories of various care providers, I was blessed by the information a woman, a neighbor of one of the facilities I was considering, provided for my consideration. I learned that facility would not be a safe option for my dad. Once more I was amazed at the way God orchestrated the events, allowing me to be in just the right place at the right time to receive this critical piece of information. It was not by chance that I encountered this person, but by God's marvelous provision. Although the facility would have met my dad's financial needs, too many red flags had surfaced, so I removed it from my list of possible options. In early May I submitted to God's will, trusting Him regarding my dad's placement and his finances. I stopped trying to control and cover every possible outcome, making myself crazy in the process. Only God knew how long my dad would live, and only God was able to meet both his needs and mine. It was then that the sense of peace returned to me. Dad moved back to the group home in mid-May, this time as a hospice patient and at a reduced rate. I thanked God for protecting Dad and being my provider, for making available the safe care setting I had already chosen at a rate that would help ease the financial burden.

One of the most difficult decisions I had to make prior to Dad's move was regarding the removal of the PEG feeding tube that had been surgically placed to improve his nutrition. The continuation of the tube would have been contrary to hospice guidelines and continuing with it would have jeopardized Dad's ability to receive hospice support. I was in a quandary over a quantity of things: the value of life, the sanctity of life at all stages, respecting Dad's wishes, and honoring my dad as directed by the fifth commandment in the Bible. The words of Exodus 20:12, which says, "Honor your father and your mother, that your days may be long upon the land which the LORD your God is giving you," guided me. One of the pastors from the church we attended offered biblical counseling and support to me during this time. I was able to voice my concerns to him about respecting Dad's wishes, helping him be as safe and comfortable as possible while doing nothing to get in the way of whatever plan God had for him. We spent time looking at scripture together, pondering the meaning, and praying for discernment. Finally, I reached the decision to proceed with the removal of the tube in mid-July. Once I did, I felt a peace that could only have come from the Lord. The weighing of pros and cons for the two options, the sense of pressure to make a choice, the fear of letting down Dad or my God were gone. There is power in God's written word that clears away confusion and makes clear the intent of the heart. The sense of peace I found came from God's word.

Dad's physical condition did not decline after the removal of the feeding tube, and he continued to receive the benefits available to him through hospice. Soon afterward there were changes in the group home policy related to DNR (orders to not resuscitate) that led to my decision to move Dad from there into a small adult foster home (AFH) in early August. As I reflect back on Dad's time at the group home I see many blessings: there were opportunities for me to share with the care providers about God's plan for the submission of both husbands and wives in marriage; I was able to tell how God freed me from alcoholism; Dad benefitted from the integrity of the nurse manager at the home; there were opportunities for me to show kindness and compassion to other residents by bringing home-baked goodies and applying fingernail polish to some of the ladies. I saw so clearly how God is in the details, even the smallest detail, when I am going through trials. It was no coincidence that my father received care from a nurse during his long hospital stay whose family owned the foster home he moved into many months later. That nurse provided strong support for both Dad and me during his hospital stay, guiding me through the complicated discharge planning, advocating for us, and keeping me updated on changes as they occurred. God's protective hand was over me, His love encompassing me as He engineered every detail of my dad's final year of life.

On the day in August my husband returned from Seoul, Dad was admitted to the hospital hospice unit due to low blood pressure and increased confusion. Two weeks later I got a phone call from a nurse early one evening regarding Dad having taken a fall and being combative to the degree the nurses were not able to attend to a cut he sustained during his fall. They knew of my ability to calm my dad and asked me to come and help him. During the drive to the hospital I talked to God, asking for the words and touch to help calm my dad. He was suspicious at first but eventually relaxed enough to share some ice cream with me as we talked. The medication the nurse had been able to mix into his portion helped to relax him, and I was soon able to leave him in their good care and return home. Dad was able to return to the foster home in early September, accompanied by a warning to me from his hospice nurse that death was near.

As I tried to be a "good wife" to Roger while maintaining a frequent presence with my dad, my stress level increased. I wanted to be available for quality time with my husband, to continue making good homemade meals and dessert treats and have adequate energy for our time together. It felt like I was robbing him of the wife time he deserved when I was devoting so much time to my dad. There was not enough of me to go around! I sometimes wished my husband's return had come later, after my dad died, and I am sure he felt my tension. At the end of September, I had a revelation regarding the heavy burden I felt: my husband was not an added burden; he was there to carry my burdens with me. From that moment on, for the remaining eight days of my dad's life, I relaxed and felt that I could focus all my time and energy on my dad. There were three of us now carrying the burden together: Jesus, my husband, and me. When I looked at the framed "Footprints in the Sand" hanging on a wall at home, an image was sharp in my mind: there was only one set of footprints at that point in time; the footprints in the sand were Christ's, and He was carrying me.

On October 14, I received a call at the Pregnancy Center early in the morning. The hospice nurse reported changes in Dad and suggested I come if I wanted to spend time with him; she sensed it might be his last day. With the prayers and blessing of my coworkers I left to spend the day with my dad. Christian music played on the radio next to his bed, as it had for months, and I read to him and talked to him about so many things from our shared past. I told him that he had always been a hard worker, taking care of Mom and me and providing us with a good home. I talked about the way his love of nature had impacted me and had led to my appreciation for the beauty of God's creation. I assured him I had a husband who loved me and would take good care of me. I gave my dad permission to let go and have his final rest and peace. On his way home from work, Roger stopped for fast food and brought it to share with me in Dad's room. He spoke to my dad, although Dad had not opened his eyes or spoken for days, saying his last goodbye. Shortly after he left, a favorite song came on the radio, "He Is Able," and I put my head on my dad's shoulder and sang along quietly. As I sang, my dad's breathing changed and he took a final, rattling breath. His heart began to beat more and more slowly, finally ceasing, as my head rested on his chest. I waited several minutes before alerting the caregiver and asked her to call hospice to let them know Dad was gone. Throughout the experience, I felt a peace and calm I cannot describe; I felt the presence of the LORD with me in the room that evening. The words of Ephesians 3:18–19, "May you be able to feel and understand, as all God's children should, how high His love really is; and to experience this love for yourselves . . . and so at last you will be filled up with God Himself," tell of God's amazing love for me. He provides what I do not deserve and cannot earn. God reveals His character and His qualities most clearly during the darkest, most difficult times in our lives.

## Chapter 7

# Spiritual Battlefield

As I recall various trials I have encountered during my years as a Christian, I see that many were not battles of human will, of flesh and blood, but spiritual battles involving unseen powers and principalities. On the surface, it seemed that there was a conflict between people, with resistance, rejection or even open hostility displayed, but the real enemy was unseen. The Book of Ephesians, chapter 6, verse 12 says, "For we do not wrestle against flesh and blood, but against principalities, against powers, against the rulers of the darkness of this age, against spiritual hosts of wickedness in the heavenly places." I found this to be the case in numerous situations: while working in a Christian workplace, at the heart of neighbor disputes, during employment with a governmental agency, and in my own marriage relationship. In each case, recognizing the enemy was the critical first step of the battle.

The primary work of the Christian workplace where I spent five years, beginning as a volunteer and later as a staff member, was to provide lay counseling and support to women who were experiencing unplanned pregnancies, counseling for hurting post-abortive women, and abstinence education in local schools. The work was supportive of human life and its great value at all stages, from conception in the womb to the end of life. The center's message was contrary to the mainstream thinking of the day, with its focus on the rights of women. That focus ignored the negative impact abortion can have on women and failed to provide help and hope for them. Many volunteers and staff were connected to the facility because of abortion choices they or loved ones had made, the rights they had exercised and later regretted, and the consequences they experienced as a result of their choice. Some of the women struggled with addictions or eating disorders while others experienced failures in the relationships they had hoped to save by not continuing a pregnancy. Others expressed the heartbreak of not being able to conceive again, living with the regret of an only child lost, while some experienced the inability to carry another child to term. The heart of the organization was to help women and girls become fully informed about abortion prior to reaching a decision and to know that post-abortion counseling was available to help them if they struggled with the aftermath of an abortion choice.

The unseen enemy is against this effort to value and preserve life. The spiritual warfare presented itself in various forms: lack of unity on organization goals, disruptive influences among volunteers or staff, physical injuries, negative media coverage, and inadequate financial support. Prayer was a key component of each shift each day the pregnancy center was open to provide services. Personally, I clung to the scripture that spoke of preparing for the spiritual battle, much as the Roman soldiers clad themselves for physical battle. Ephesians chapter 6, verses 12–18 speak of "putting on the armor of God in order to withstand the evil day." Each physical piece of clothing mentioned represents a part of the spiritual preparation that is necessary: "the belt of truth, the breastplate of righteousness, the shoes for the gospel of peace, the shield of faith, the helmet of salvation and the sword representing the power of God's word." Going into battle without the physical protection would have been foolhardy; failing to put on the spiritual armor leaves one vulnerable to the assaults of the enemy, as well.

During one particularly difficult period at work I awoke with a start from a bad dream in the middle of the night. In the dream lions were on the loose, biting and killing people all around them in a small village. A little girl had run outside when it seemed the area was clear, then she crouched down close to a small, single-story building just as one lion suddenly appeared. She was in a squatting position, leaning forward with her arms bent tight against her chest and her hands held up to her face. The lion nearly passed by, then circled over to her and began sniffing at the back of her head and neck. At that point I felt panic welling up inside me, with a prickling feeling running up my back and shoulders, tensing as the lion sniffed the motionless little girl. When the lion started nibbling on the back of her neck it seemed

*Finding Hope*

I felt something on the back of my neck, like teeth or claws pressing against me. I awoke abruptly, sensing that the lion had bitten into the child's neck and broken her spinal cord although I did not see it in the dream. As I talked with my husband about the bad dream, I recognized the lion symbolism from the Book of 1 Peter 5: 8–9: "Be sober, be vigilant; because your adversary the devil walks about like a roaring lion, seeking whom he may devour. Resist him, steadfast in the faith, knowing that the same sufferings are experienced by your brotherhood in the world." The little girl in the dream represented me and my vulnerability to spiritual warfare; it was a stark reminder of the need for spiritual preparation every single day.

Spiritual warfare and prayer were ever present in the Christian workplace. As a nonprofit organization, financial survival depended on the generous support of faithful supporters, with two annual events, one a walk for life and the other a silent auction fundraiser, providing the primary funding for the year. Each volunteer, donor, and employee had a heart for the work of the organization, and each had personal expectations or preferences for how the work should be accomplished and what the long-term and immediate goals should be. Some favored additional counseling centers and incorporating ultrasound capability at the centers, others hoped to increase resources for adoption services, and yet others felt the greatest accomplishment would come through increasing the school abstinence training program. There were disappointments and sometimes resentments formed when the final goals for the organization did not coincide with individual preferences. Whenever there was disgruntlement or a disruptive influence apparent in the centers, I knew that Satan was at work trying to harm the organization. When that happened, I turned to prayer: "Lord, let us see the hearts that seek to do Your good work. Help us to discern what is true and to reject the lies of the enemy who seeks to destroy the work of this ministry. Protect the staff and volunteers and grant them wisdom as they speak truth to the girls, women and students who are our clients. Find us faithful in prayer and thanksgiving and allow all we say and do to honor You."

Spiritual attack comes in many ways, sometimes in the form of injury or sickness, in ways that threaten fundraising or training efforts. In one instance a motor vehicle accident impacted all of these: it prevented a key person in the organization from speaking to potential donors at an evening event and eliminated the main presenter for the upcoming volunteer training seminar. Prayers began immediately upon hearing news of the accident: for recovery of the injured, preparation for those who would fill in for the injured person, and that the ministry would be strengthened by the very thing that Satan intended for harm. I personally experienced God's faithfulness as He equipped me to lead the training seminar in place of the injured worker. This responsibility came ahead of the planned timing for me to assume the lead role in volunteer training. The person injured in the accident was in the process of mentoring me to assume that role, and although I had not led some of the sessions previously, God gave me the words to speak each day of the seminar. I was not adequately prepared, yet God was able to use me provided I was willing and trusted Him. It would have been easy for me to be overwhelmed by the presence of my injured mentor and my immediate supervisor. Given my pattern of being easily intimidated by authority figures, having two of them in the room listening to most of my presentation was stressful. If I had focused on me, comparing my style and presentation to my mentor, it would have been detrimental. I focused instead on scripture that reminded me of God's provision. Bits and pieces of His word ran through my mind as I organized material before the training sessions: He has given me a sound mind; He has not given me a spirit of fear; He has prepared me to do a good work and will provide the words I need for the occasion. Spiritual attack can come in so many ways, often when I least expect it. If there had been more time for me to prepare, I might not have relied so heavily on the Lord and would have depended on my own strength. This situation let me see my inadequacy and His great power. When my trust is in the Lord and I keep my eyes fixed on Him, He will always make a way.

As I recall two neighborhood situations, I can see clearly that our marriage relationship and our home were the targets of Satan's attack on us. The first occurrence began the year I lived alone in Oregon while Roger fulfilled a final one-year commitment with his Arizona employer. It seemed initially to be a routine land-use issue. We had purchased a peaceful home on the North Umpqua River at the end of 1999, with a large ranch property west of us across the river and a vacant field adjacent to us on the north, the downriver side of our property. The realtor had told us there would be no building on the vacant field due to an easement related to that property, so we envisioned privacy and quiet in our country setting. Our view to the west and north included rolling hills, grassy fields interspersed with oak trees and scrub brush, and lots of blue sky on a clear day. Herons occasionally waded along the shoreline, and bald eagles soared overhead, searching the clear river water for fish. During a visit to our property the following summer we saw a gravel drive had been installed on the adjacent lot, winding from the higher elevation of the long, narrow lot down to the river's edge. We were concerned. Several neighbors reported seeing signs of commercial fishing activity from the property, adding to our level of stress. The following fall I moved into our country home and became the conveyor of bad news to my husband as I saw changes on the lot next to us. It grieved me to tell him I had seen bulldozers at work and what appeared to be the beginning of a building pad. We tried to find some written documentation of the view easement so we could halt the construction but with no success. It seemed our peaceful Oregon dream was vanishing before our eyes, and there might be no recourse to stop it. Even though I shared the loss of peace Roger felt, I sensed this was something more than a battle between us and our neighbor. Satan was involved in what we were experiencing; it was spiritual warfare. If our spiritual enemy could create division between us over the issue, rob us of the joy we initially felt upon seeing our home for the first time, or cause us to behave in ways that would shame Christ, Satan would do that.

One of my daily devotions in *The Best of Andrew Murray on Prayer* spoke to me, and I felt a strong conviction to persevere in prayer for our neighbor as well as for us. It was not easy or natural to do this, and I struggled against it initially as I committed time daily to pray aloud and seek God's help. It is easy to pray for people we like, for those going through difficulties that arouse in us a sense of compassion, a desire to protect, or some other positive response. It can be difficult to pray for the benefit of someone who seems to be hurting us, is putting obstacles in our path that will keep us from accomplishing our goals, or is in some other way negatively impacting our lives. Yet, Jesus says in Matthew 6:44, "But I say to you, love your enemies, bless those who curse you, do good to those who hate you, and pray for those who spitefully use you and persecute you." I could not see a way out of the situation, one that would benefit the neighbor and us, but I knew that being obedient to God meant praying for my neighbor, and I continued to pray.

Throughout the fall and spring months, peak times for fishing along the beautiful river, I took photos of boat launches from the adjacent lot and shared the information with the County Planning Department, the entity already investigating a potential zoning violation on that property. That summer I was asked by them to testify at a trial regarding the issue. In preparation, I asked God to give me the words to speak and to reveal truth regarding the situation. Scripture gave me comfort and focus, especially the words of Philippians 4:13: "I can do all things through Christ who strengthens me." God was a faithful provider, equipping me with words, strength, and peace prior to and during the trial. A month later we learned the details of another neighbor's view and river easement: it provided protection to them by prohibiting building on the lower level of the lot next to us, benefiting us as well as them. There was no commercial fishing activity during the peak seasons that followed, yet I knew that the issue would not be fully resolved until the neighbor was able to sell the property. Since there would be no income from commercial fishing from the property, it would present a financial burden to him. My prayers during that time were focused on God providing a way for this neighbor to be released from that burden. I had no idea what that would look like or when it might occur. The following year the neighbor was able to sell the property to a person who had no commercial interest and would use the boat launch solely for personal purposes. We could not have predicted the timing or the nature of the provision from God. It reinforced for me the good that can come from being faithful to pray for others, even those who seem to be my enemy. What Satan had intended for harm, God was able to use to draw me closer to Him and to strengthen me for battles that were yet to come.

The second neighbor dispute was related to noise, the disruption of peace in general, and eventually the lack of restful sleep for my husband, the result of a rooster crowing at various hours, both day and night. Over a four-year span the problems escalated between my husband and this neighbor, culminating in a two-year civil lawsuit, trial, and jury verdict. The behaviors exhibited by both men were part of a spiritual battle that raged throughout those years. The self-wills and rights of both men took on a power that was not easily explained. It appeared no compromise or agreement could be reached that would satisfy them and restore peace to the neighborhood. My husband seemed obsessed by the conflict to the point that nothing else seemed to matter. As a believer in Christ, he had the power of the Holy Spirit working in him, giving him the ability to live his life in obedience to God. Yet, he could still respond, as any believer can, in the same way he would have prior to trusting Jesus. The conflict between a believer's desire to respond in a Christlike manner and the power of old habits and patterns, the flesh, is real. Recognizing the spiritual battle going on was what allowed me to pray for him, continue to love him, and speak truth to him in love even at the hardest times. At my lowest point I feared there might be no limit to the sacrifice made, perhaps even our marriage, to win this battle. Satan was at work seeking to destroy our marriage as never before. In the depth of my pain and despair I could still see that Satan was the enemy, not my husband or our neighbor, and I knew that only God could provide a way through the ugly maze.

As we went through the years of turmoil related to this neighbor issue, only God had the power to change us, to bring something beautiful out of the ashes. We were not in agreement on how to handle the problem, our ways of communicating with our neighbors were different, and we were not united in our focus. He was focused on the neighbor problem while I was focused on displaying Christlikeness as we went through our trial. Throughout the years, I cried out to God. I cried for my heart to be changed: for the ability to love my husband no matter how things went, to not fall back into a pattern of resentment and bitterness toward him, and to forgive him over the hurts I felt. I cried out that my husband would be changed: for his heart to be softened, for him to hear God speak to him, for him to glorify Christ with his behaviors, for him to value our marriage above the battle, and for him to forgive as he has been forgiven by God.

At one point I pleaded for God to bring us over, under, or around the ordeal, yet He chose to bring us through it. The way was not easy, and I did not know if I could endure the prolonged strain. At the end of the civil trial our attorney said he had doubted our marriage would survive the ordeal, but it did. Our marriage remains intact; it is stronger now. We grew in our ability to communicate with each other: I stopped being afraid of making him angry and learned to speak what was needed when I would not have in the past. He began to hear not just the words I spoke but to also understand my good intention as I shared difficult things with him. God allowed me to support my husband even though I was not in agreement with his endeavor.

My preparation for this spiritual battle came from fourteen years of daily Bible reading, numerous teachings from local pastors, reading devotional books, participating in women's Bible study groups and other Christian training sessions. I understood that, as a child of God, I was being conformed to the image of Christ, and my behaviors were to reflect that. That greatly influenced my approach to handling conflicts, no matter where I encountered them. My focus was on maintaining a right walk with God while working through the issue with my neighbor and being respectful of my husband. Because my relationship with God mattered more to me than any specific detail required for resolution, I did not have the same level of investment in a particular outcome that my husband had. This created tension between us, with it seeming at times to him that I was not being supportive, when in fact I was. Throughout the ordeal I recognized my husband as the head of our household, providing him with information that could help him reach a decision, speaking truth about potential outcomes and costs, yet yielding the final decision making to him. While I was not supportive of the decision to file a civil suit, one could not legally be pursued without my written agreement, so I supported my husband by giving it. I feared the failure to do so would create a wedge of resentment between us that would be difficult to overcome. My prayers were still for divine intervention that would eliminate the need for a trial. When no acceptable resolution was found prior to the trial date, despite my reluctance, I took the witness stand first to provide the groundwork needed by our attorney to present the case to the jurors.

On many occasions during the years of conflict I clung to God's word, finding comfort, strength, and hope in what I read. One of the Andrew Murray devotions was especially powerful: "Disregard the workings of your own will and reason. Then you will know the power and love of God in its fullness."[2] My fears, worries, timing, and plan for resolution had to give way so that I could know God's power and love. At one point, Roger suggested in a note he left for me that he could move out of our home until the trial was over, desiring to not add to my burden. How could he possibly think that my burden would be lessened by him living somewhere else? Such a thought could only come out of the spiritual battle that swirled around us. I envisioned God by my side as I read Psalm 23:4: "Yea, though I walk through the valley of the shadow of death, I will fear no evil; for You are with me; Your rod and Your staff, they comfort me." I knew then that there would be no easy way out of our dilemma, but I also trusted that God was with me and would not forsake me. When he came home from work that evening, I told him moving out was not an option, nor was losing our marriage to Satan, and we would somehow manage to get through the challenge together. In the past I would have given up, run away, or withdrawn from the cause of my pain. In this case, I recognized the spiritual battle and knew the real source of my pain was not my spouse. To my amazement, I learned to be content in the center of the fiery trial, desiring Christlikeness and accepting God's will for my life. The words from 1 Timothy 6:6, "Now godliness with contentment is great gain," became real for me in the coming months.

Throughout the four years, God was faithful to protect me from my old pattern of bitterness and resentment. In their place came hurt, loss and grief, a burden that God alone was able to relieve over time. I experienced hurt when it seemed my husband could not see the situation from my perspective, no matter how often or plainly I tried to communicate it to him. This was made worse when I considered he might understand yet still be choosing to move ahead with the legal action against our neighbor, at all costs. It seemed he was choosing the harlot of revenge over our marriage. A flesh-and-blood woman might have been an easier adversary to combat than this spiritual opponent. My sense of loss was related to the dream we had shared for community with neighbors amidst the beautiful, peaceful, country setting. That was gone, irretrievably broken, and the refreshment I had once felt in

---

[2] A. Murray, *The Best of Andrew Murray on Prayer* (Uhrichsville, OH: Barbour Publishing, Inc., 1996) August 14.

my home was no longer there. I spent long hours at my demanding job, fifty to sixty hours per week, without the sense of a safe place to return to at the end of a hard day. The grief came to me as I saw the sweet side of my husband swallowed up in revenge. His heart seemed hardened, even toward me at times. My heart ached for him while I cried out to God for help. Rays of hope shown through the strain, however, as he began to rely more and more on scripture to help him through difficult times in the legal preparation. Prior to the jury's verdict, I prayed to God, acknowledging our sins that had been revealed, thanking God for hearing my cries for forgiveness, and asking for His mercy. When the jury ruled against us on all the claims brought against our neighbor, my heart hurt anew for my husband. The decision was not unexpected for me, but it seemed to take him completely by surprise. A separate settlement between us and our neighbors was reached at the direction of the judge that restored a measure of quiet to the neighborhood, but the division between neighbors remained.

The following day I wrote in my journal, "Though He slay me, yet will I trust Him." Those words from Job 13:15 expressed the attitude of my heart toward God, the One who had brought me through a prolonged spiritual battle. With each delay, discouragement, or wave of worry my reliance on Him increased. Like Job, a just man who lost wealth, family, and health as a result of Satan's influence on his life, I had suffered much, yet grown in my faith. My trust grew as I relied more and more on God throughout the years, and I repeatedly experienced His faithful provision for me. The financial costs related to the legal action were significant, the strain on our marital relationship, including lost intimacy and joyful moments, was costly; the physical and emotional strain for such a prolonged period impacted both of us. God's marvelous provision came in so many ways: His small whisper directing me to just the right scripture to encourage me in the middle of the night, a pastor available to listen and pray with me on the phone at one of my lowest points, the beauty of a sunset on my drive home at the end of a long workday.

The enemy was powerful, but he did not overcome me. I recognized my real enemy early in my trials and put on the armor of God to withstand the evil day. I resisted the enemy, standing steadfast in faith. On every spiritual battlefield God was faithful!

# Chapter 8

## *Rejecting The Lies*

As I look back over the years, I see clearly patterns of negative behavior precipitated by my emotional reactions to the circumstances of life. An unkind word from a coworker or family member, rejection by an employer for a position I sought, or failure to achieve a certain grade or performance evaluation at work could throw me into emotional turmoil for days. Sometimes I raged, sometimes I was hard on myself, critical of my looks, ability, or some other facet. My responses were reactive and emotionally charged during the years before I accepted Christ. Even after I began my Christian walk, I continued to experience the sting of criticism, even when kindly given, but my responses began to change. The quick retort, angry tone, and looks, the vulgar words I had used in the past were gone. Instead, I found myself withdrawing physically or emotionally, sometimes both, as I processed what had happened. I began to seek God's word regarding what I was feeling and learned to confess to Him the anger, resentment, or bitterness I was experiencing. My desire was to please God, but some things still seemed to trigger negative feelings, trapping me in the old patterns that seemed inconsistent with my new freedom in Christ.

As I read Robert McGee's book, *The Search for Significance*, it was obvious I had fallen in the past for the lies of the great deceiver, Satan, and I continued to be triggered by them even as a believer. Perhaps the greatest deception for me was the one about my worth. For years I thought my worth was something I had to earn, and I measured it by other people's approval of me. McGee summarized the lie well in this formula: "My Self Worth = Performance + Others' Opinions."[3] It was not hard to recall the many ways I had attempted to feel better about myself, by pleasing others and seeking their approval and acceptance, yet it was painful taking a close look at the feelings that were triggered when I failed. My effort to get good grades at every level of education, being critical of my own accomplishments, comparing myself to others, altering my looks surgically, and using my sensuality in a manipulative way were all indications of my great need for approval. I wrongly believed that if I performed well, then I would have the approval of others and would be able to feel good about myself. So long as I believed Satan's lie about my worth, no amount of approval from others would ever be enough. Each time I fell short in some sense, missed the mark I had set for myself, I would be subject to the fear of failure, feelings of shame, inferiority, and hopelessness. Recognizing the lies, as McGee indicated, was the first step in breaking out of the cycle. Real freedom could only come from rejecting the lies and replacing them with God's truth.

The truth about my worth is found in God's word, not in the approval of the world. As John 1:12 says, "But as many as received Him, to them He gave the right to become children of God, to those who believe in His name." As a believer, I am a daughter of the King. What greater worth could I desire? In the words of 2 Corinthians 5:17, "If anyone is in Christ, he is a new creation; old things have passed away; behold, all things have become new." The old habits and patterns have lost their power over me; I am no longer a slave to Satan and his lies. Romans 6:17–18 says, "But God be thanked that though you were slaves of sin, yet you obeyed from the heart that form of doctrine to which you were delivered. And having been set free from sin, you became slaves of righteousness." I believed the Gospel message: Jesus died for my sin and rose again from the grave. Jesus not only accepted me just as I was, He loves me so much that He is changing me to become more like Him. Second Corinthians 3:18 says, "But we all, with unveiled face, beholding as in a mirror the glory of the Lord, are being transformed into the same image from glory to glory, just

---

[3] R.S, McGee, *The Search for Significance, Book and Workbook* (Nashville, TN: W Publishing Group, 1998) 22.

*Finding Hope*

as by the Spirit of the Lord." My endless striving has ended, and I can rest, knowing that the Lord has accepted me just as I am. I no longer need to perform to be approved by others or be acceptable to myself; my worth is found in Christ alone.

Another of Satan's lies plagued me, continuing into the early phase of my Christian walk: You are a loser; you cannot change. It manifested itself in feelings of hopelessness when my first two marriages ended in divorce and during my years of heavy drinking. The downward spiral, my second marriage failing sooner than the first, my failed efforts to control my drinking, and the increase in alcohol-related black outs over the years all fed the lie and my fear that I would never break free, that I could not change. Feelings of shame began early for me, fueled by the loss of my virginity, my adultery in my first marriage, my decision to leave my children with their dad when we divorced, and haunting recollections of my behavior toward others during the darkest years of my life. It was not until I began writing this book that I finally came to see the awful truth: I had *abandoned* my children. When marriage didn't go as I had hoped it would, when I still felt insignificant and unloved, I left everything behind, and I ran away. For years I had denied the truth, putting my actions in more positive terms. Until then I had been able to cling to the story of a mother looking out for the needs of her children at the time of a divorce, not allowing them to be separated from one another but sacrificing so that they could be raised in one home, in this case with their dad. I had avoided labeling my past action with such a negative term for years, calling it what it truly was, but I knew what I had done was wrong, and I experienced shame.

In his chapter on shame, McGee talks about the relationship between performance-based worth and past behavior. "We then have unconsciously incorporated Satan's lie into our belief system: I must always be what I have been and live with whatever self-worth I have because that's just me."[4] My negative past behaviors did become, in my own mind, what determined my worth. The only way for me to stop being triggered by feelings of shame was to reject Satan's lie and replace it with God's word. The words of King David in Psalm 32, verses 3–5,

---

[4] R.S, McGee, *The Search for Significance, Book and Workbook* (Nashville, TN: W Publishing Group, 1998) 266.

speak powerfully to me: "When I kept silent, my bones grew old through my groaning all the day long. For day and night Your hand was heavy upon me; my vitality was turned into the drought of summer. I acknowledged my sin to You, and my iniquity I have not hidden. I said, 'I will confess my transgressions to the LORD,' and You forgave the iniquity of my sin." When I kept silent, before I acknowledged my sin and my need for a relationship with God, I was consumed by shame. The longer I delayed my confession, the more my feelings of worthlessness and hopelessness grew. That weight was lifted as I confessed, and I experienced the joy of forgiveness, just as David had. One of Oswald Chamber's daily devotions says, "Never be afraid when God brings back your past. Let your memory have its way with you. It is a minister of God bringing its rebuke and sorrow to you. God will turn what might have been into a wonderful lesson of growth for the future."[5] When I recall this dark time from my past, I experience sadness and regret; there is sorrow. However, the sense of shame has been removed.

The words of 2 Corinthians 5:17, "Therefore, if anyone is in Christ, he is a new creation; old things have passed away; behold, all things have become new," were so powerful. God's word says I am not the same person I once was. The old behaviors, the old desires, the downward spirals from my past no longer define me. In Romans 8:1 the apostle Paul says, "There is therefore now no condemnation to those who are in Christ Jesus, who do not walk according to the flesh, but according to the Spirit." Paul's message applies to me; I have believed in Jesus and will not come under the judgment that decides eternal destiny. Before Jesus was crucified, He told His disciples that He was going away but would send them a Helper, the Holy Spirit. John 16:8–11 says, "And when He has come, He will convict the world of sin, and of righteousness, and of judgment: of sin, because they do not believe in Me; of righteousness, because I go to My Father and you see Me no more; of judgment, because the ruler of this world is judged." In the Oswald Chamber's devotional book, *My Utmost for His Highest*, it says, "Condemnation comes when I realize that Jesus Christ came to

---

[5] James Reimann, ed., *My Utmost for His Highest* (Grand Rapids, MI: Discovery House Publishers, 1992) April 3.

deliver me from this heredity of sin, and yet I refuse to let Him do so."[6] Christ delivered me from my heredity of sin on February 11, 1990. His Spirit continues to work in my life, convicting me of unrighteousness and developing Christlikeness in me. In the Book of John, chapter 5, verse 24, Jesus spoke reassurance to His disciples: "Most assuredly, I say to you, he who hears My word and believes in Him who sent Me has everlasting life, and shall not come into judgment, but has passed from death into life." The power of God's word cannot be denied; my shame has been removed by the cleansing of Christ's blood shed on the Cross of Calvary.

Discerning the difference between God's good gifts and Satan's temptations can be difficult. For years I thought that if something was beautiful, good, or pleasurable I deserved it and should have it. There was a sense of entitlement without any sense of restraint, without considering the consequences of my actions. I was often drawn away in pursuit of what tempted me, to the exclusion of other things and people. This was one of the lies I came to reject as I matured spiritually. God created humans, male and female, and gave them the ability to desire each other physically. He provided guidelines for using this gift wisely and prohibitions against certain practices. When I engaged in sexual activity outside of marriage, I moved beyond the realm of God's intention for good in my life and into the area of sinful sensual pleasures. First John 2:16 says, "For all that is in the world—the lust of the flesh, the lust of the eyes, and the pride of life—is not of the Father but of the world." Any of the natural desires God has given, when taken to extremes, can lead to sin. Having an attractive home, wearing nice clothing, or having a job with a title do not necessarily indicate sin in a person's life. If the desire for these things is so strong that the person's focus is on them instead of God, that is an indication the person has been caught up in the lust of the world. James 1:14–15 says, "But each one is tempted when he is drawn away by his own desires and enticed. Then, when desire has conceived, it gives birth to sin; and sin, when it is full-grown, brings forth death." God's word sustains me and helps me overcome Satan's lie: I am entitled to all that is in the world.

---

[6] James Reimann, ed., *My Utmost for His Highest* (Grand Rapids, MI: Discovery House Publishers, 1992) October 5.

I am aware now of the way I can be easily enticed, and I know that the enticement to sin does not come from God. For James 1:13 says, "Let no one say when he is tempted, 'I am tempted by God'; for God cannot be tempted by evil, nor does He Himself tempt anyone." I can enjoy God's good gifts to me without thinking I am entitled to all that is in the world. I am equipped to reject the lie that would tempt me to sin.

During my reading of *The Screwtape Letters* by C.S. Lewis I gained additional insight into the many subtle ways Satan works in a believer's life to draw him away from reliance on God and relationship with Him. In chapter three Lewis describes the many ways Satan works in close relationships, like marriage, injecting daily pinpricks that damage the relationship and take the believer's eyes off God. I realized my focus on my husband's spiritual development during our early Christian years, comparing his spiritual maturity to mine, resulted in irritation toward him and some degree of disconnect between us. That behavior, left unchecked, would lead to pride in my life and could keep me from maturing spiritually. Lewis describes the dynamics between a woman and the adult son who lives with her. The son focuses on the way his mother lifts her eyebrows, something "he learned to dislike in the nursery."[7] Under the influence of a demon, he assumes "that she knows how annoying it is and does it to annoy . . . he will not notice the immense improbability of the assumption."[8] The demon also keeps the son from seeing that he has tones and looks that are annoying to his mother. As I read, I saw that my annoyance with a few of my husband's facial expressions or tones of voice had kept me from seeing my own faults. Some of my expressions and tone of voice had to be equally annoying to him. My oversensitivity and speculation about my husband's intention when he did these things were a result of Satan's influence, creating a double standard. In Lewis's book, one demon instructs another: "Hence from every quarrel they can go away convinced, or very nearly convinced, that they are quite innocent . . . Once this habit is well established you have the delightful situation of a human saying things with the express purpose of offending and yet having a grievance when

---

[7] C.S. Lewis, *The Screwtape Letters* (New York, NY: Simon & Schuster Inc., 1996) 26.

[8] Ibid. 26.

offence is taken."[9] Satan had attempted to divert me in my Christian walk in even the simplest daily interactions with my husband. The fabrication of a double standard had put a wedge between us. I recalled the time we worked together installing storm doors, four of them, in our coastal home. Roger's facial expression was somber, he spoke little, and his voice conveyed irritation when he did speak. I interpreted what was happening as irritation with me over the way I was helping or some unspoken issue. I was afraid to offer any suggestion, was awkward in handing him pieces, and wishing the project was over when it had barely begun. We talked about the storm door project later ,and I learned he had no frustration with me but was extremely frustrated with the written instructions that came with the doors, as well as with himself at his ability, and that led to irritation. Although I had read his emotion correctly, I was completely off base regarding the reason; it had nothing to do with me! How could I have so missed the mark? My own childhood experiences, living with a dad who often wore a stern facial expression, a muscle that would twitch in his neck as he seemed deep in thought, and admonitions from Mom not to bother my dad when he looked like that played a part. I began to ask for more information or inquire about my husband's well-being when I saw an expression or heard a tone of voice that I would have previously interpreted as negative or hurtful. I stopped assuming he was being critical of me; I began trusting that he had my well-being in mind. It was amazing how quickly the old triggers lost their power, and it became much easier to sense Satan's hand in things. Recognizing that influence and processing events in the light of God's word, knowing His intent for good in my life, was critical to developing strong relationships with both my husband and God.

Jesus said, in John 10:10, "The thief does not come except to steal, and to kill, and to destroy. I have come that they may have life, and that they may have it more abundantly." The thief is Satan; he comes with evil intention, not to benefit me. When he sows discord in my marriage, he is seeking to steal my joy, to put out the flame of love that exists between me and my husband, and to destroy the covenantal relationship that God has blessed. There is no intent in my heart I can hide

---

[9] Ibid. 26–27.

from God. First Chronicles 28:9 says, "The LORD searches all hearts and understands all the intent of the thoughts. If you seek Him, He will be found by you; but if you forsake Him, He will cast you off forever." God cares for me, and I have access to Him; all I need to do is seek Him, as I do with my prayers and praise. The instruction in James 4:7 is clear: "Therefore submit to God. Resist the devil and he will flee from you." God has given me the ability to recognize the devil's lies more quickly. I am now alert to his subtle influence, and I am relying on Jesus daily to keep me walking in the light with Him. Real freedom comes from rejecting the lies and replacing them with God's truth.

CHAPTER 9

## Ample Provision

THROUGHOUT THE YEARS I HAVE SEEN REPEATEDLY THE way God provides for me, often meeting my needs just in the nick of time, opening my eyes to unseen possibilities, providing blessings even as I go through the difficulties. Perhaps the greatest example of His provision can be seen in the years I refer to as our "Oregon adventure." In the fall of 1999, Roger and I began an adventure that would take us from the heavily populated hot, dry desert of Arizona to somewhere cooler and more rural in the northwest. Both of us had grown up in the eastern United States, living in areas that experienced four seasons, and we knew our ability to tolerate the extremes in weather. It seemed to us that the long, hot summer of Phoenix became a little hotter and a little longer each year. As we aged, the extreme heat seemed to take more of a toll on us, and we longed for what we recalled as the best climate from our childhood years. We planned to begin our search along Interstate 5 in Oregon, stopping in towns and cities between Portland on the north end and Ashland on the south end of the I-5 corridor, over a nine-day period. As we began our search, there was no timeline in mind for relocating, just the desire to see what options Oregon offered.

Beginning the very first day of our journey, I saw how our vacillating emotions, moving up and down like a yo-yo as the events of the day unfolded, contrasted with God's plan and goodness for us. He has a plan for us and knows everything each day will bring before the day begins. He is steadfast in all His ways and not subject to the emotional ups and downs human beings experience throughout the day. During the early morning shuttle ride from our home to the airport, I experienced God's protective hand over me. When another passenger boarded the shuttle at a hotel along the way to the airport, the reek of alcohol hit my nostrils, triggering memories of the times I had partied hard at night and oozed alcohol vapors from my pores the next morning. It amazed me to experience the great power of this olfactory trigger and the resulting waves of nausea I battled while the man stretched out to sleep on the seat behind me. Not only had alcohol lost the strong appeal it once had in my life, now the lingering scent of stale alcohol could at times be repulsive to me. That kind of protection could only come from God!

Our yo-yo experience continued at the airline ticket counter, where we learned the morning flight that had presented plenty of opportunities for stand-by passengers had been cancelled. This was the first stand-by experience for us, and we had planned the remainder of the day around what had initially seemed to us such a sure thing. We waited anxiously for an afternoon flight that seemed to offer little hope to stand-by travelers. The expression on my husband's face when the attendant called our names, the last to be called for stand-by, was priceless. He looked like a little kid who had just received an unexpected gift. Once we arrived at our destination, the Portland airport, we had no trouble connecting with our luggage that had arrived on an earlier flight. We reflected at bedtime on the way God had been in all the details throughout the day: getting the last two seats on a flight that appeared initially to be fully booked, having comfortable aisle seats across from each other, and being able to locate our undamaged luggage so easily when we had been separated from it for so long. We felt God's goodness and knew that He had been in control of every detail throughout the day. God had been steadfast in His plan for us even when we despaired over our loss of control.

In the following days we checked out many towns along the southern portion of I-5, gathering information from local realtors and driving through various neighborhoods to get a feel for each area. We discovered that the rural feel was appealing to both of us, but acreage was not a necessity. When we headed north to Roseburg, we expected to check out a winery or two and drive through the surrounding small towns as we passed through. It seemed God had other plans for us, however, and we ended up spending a day and a half looking at homes listed for sale. There was one house on the North Umpqua River that the realtor offered to show us but was unable to because of the poor cell phone connection in the area when she attempted to reach the listing realtor. We dismissed that home, thinking it was probably too small based on the exterior view, and we headed north to Eugene with plans to explore some of the small towns south of there during the next day or two.

Two nights later we sat in our Eugene motel room comparing pros and cons from the homes on our list and came to the realization that the little unseen home on the North Umpqua River had the greatest potential. It met our criteria best, even though we had not seen the inside of the house. We contacted the Roseburg realtor by phone to share our interest in looking at the home and made plans to meet her the next morning. As we approached the driveway to the river home, there were four deer grazing in the meadow next to it. When the realtor opened the front door to greet us and we walked in, all I could say was, "It's gorgeous!" The river view from the great room, the size and layout of the rooms, a large wooden deck, and stone-front fireplace all spoke to us. As we stood on the deck enjoying the view and country feel, a large flock of geese flew down river, honking in unison as we looked up. A few minutes later the flock circled back and flew upriver past us. Seeing the beautiful display once was special; seeing the geese in flight a second time seemed like a wonderful gift from God. We returned to Phoenix the next day, filled with excitement at the possibilities that were ahead of us.

We knew without a doubt that Oregon was where we wanted to live; the remaining questions were where and when? Our final selection was the Roseburg house on the river, and the timing was now, at least in terms of purchasing. At that time, we thought that our physical move would be three to five years in the future, yet we knew that God's plans could be different than our plans. There was a flurry of activity: purchase offer, rejection, and counteroffers, with momentary thoughts about simply throwing in the towel and giving up on the whole thing. We felt the hand of God in the process, as if He was our guide when it came to the price of our counteroffer. When God spoke to David and His people in Psalm 32:8, He said, "I will instruct you and teach you in the way you should go; I will guide you with My eye," and in a similar way God guided us with the details of this transition. I realized much of what I struggled with during the real estate process was pride.

I had not gotten my way with the initial price we offered, although I thought I would be able to because of negotiating skills I had learned as a salesperson. After Roger went to bed one night I talked to God and asked for direction. Before I went to bed, I had a real sense of peace about counteroffering a certain amount and I wrote it on a piece of paper for my husband to consider in the morning. When he came to breakfast the next morning, he told me he had also found peace about the amount to offer. He told me the amount he had in mind before looking at what I had written the night before. We were in complete agreement on the amount for the counteroffer! The buyer accepted our offer, and we continued with the purchase of the river home. When it came to the long-distance closing on the house, my role was supportive while his was primary. He scrambled to close ahead of the deadline so the interest lock-rate we had secured would not expire, saving us about 1 percent on the loan. At times it seemed the pieces were falling apart, not coming together no matter how hard we tried, and Roger grimaced when he received a page from one of the people who was involved in the funding process. Given my generally optimistic outlook, I suggested she might be calling to let him know it was all done. What a relief to hear that was the good news she called to share. The funding on the loan was completed on December 6, nine days ahead of the closing deadline, with one hour to spare on the favorable interest lock-rate. We knew that such perfect timing, coming right down to the wire, was a very good gift from God. Trusting in God brings blessings; relying on my own strength leads to consequences. We recalled the words of Jeremiah 29:11, "For I know the plans I have for you, says the Lord. They are plans for good and not for disaster, to give you a future and a hope" (NLT).

    We celebrated the end of the year with a trip to our new Oregon home, flying into the Portland airport and driving a rental car, the "Rat-Car" as we named it (cramped, noisy, but affordable) to Roseburg. We were to meet the realtor the following morning to take possession of the keys and a bag of home documents and instructions from the previous owner. Our front door was decorated with large green and white bows and ribbon, and there was a gift basket and festive holiday plates and cups on the kitchen counter awaiting our arrival. What a wonderful welcome to our Oregon dream home! During our first visit we ordered a refrigerator, with delivery not available during our short stay, and were blessed by garage temperatures cool enough to keep our few perishable items from spoiling. We appreciated the kindness and helpful nature of the small-town salespeople as we navigated our "to do" list: apple pie and balloons from the loan office, knowledgeable but not pushy help from a salesman at Sears, and good interactions with a lawn care person. We saw squirrels and deer often during our short stay, and I could already see how much I was going to enjoy working in my kitchen, with a clear view of the river and rolling hills visible through the great room window on one side and a green hill that seemed to invite deer to graze through the smaller window looking on the opposite side. We experienced God's provision throughout our first trip to our Oregon dream home.

Our next trip to Oregon in early springtime was by car, a rental van we filled with items that would make our visits more enjoyable. We had loaded in folding camp chairs, boxes with basic dishes, pots and pans, and some clothing we would leave at our Oregon home. During a stop for gas in California around midnight, a young woman asked us for money and became pushy when we refused to give her any, threatening to call her gang. As we drove away, we were anxious and kept glancing around to see if we were being followed. Later we discussed all the things we had done wrong and saw the experience as an eye-opener that heightened our awareness of safety for future encounters in unfamiliar places, especially at night. We had stopped for gas in a deserted area, parked at the pump farthest from the building where payments were made, and had not looked around carefully before getting out of our vehicle. We knew God had been our protector that night despite our carelessness. We took turns napping and driving and reached our dream home in just over twenty-two hours. Brightly colored tulips and daffodils bloomed in our front yard, leaves were budding on the birch trees, and temperatures were in the low seventies upon arrival. There had been deer along the country road as we neared our home, and we watched a pair of geese fly overhead as we stood on the deck. We marveled at the beauty of God's creation all around us. During our stay we met several neighbors during walks along the country road, enjoyed hospitality at one couple's home, and enjoyed interacting with two dog owners and their pets. Roger submitted a job application with one local company, knowing it would be weeks before he would hear anything regarding job opportunities. It was hard leaving our Oregon home and the different lifestyle we had found there. We left with greater motivation to find employment in Oregon so we could move there sooner rather than later.

In late June we drove again to Roseburg with the intention of doing some interior painting and enjoying refreshment around the interviews my husband had scheduled with two local companies. Two disappointments greeted us immediately upon arrival at our river home: a yard full of weeds and brown grass patches plus signs of future building on the vacant field next door. Our priorities quickly changed, with irrigation troubleshooting, and weed pulling moving to the top of our list. The interviews went well with both companies, with one company seeming to be a better fit for somebody with my husband's electrical engineering background. A month later we returned for his second interview with that company, did more lawn maintenance, and continued with the interior painting. This time multiple engineers and board members were involved in the interview process, and he was invited to return for a third interview, which occurred a few days later, on the day we were to depart for Arizona. We were in a somewhat celebratory mood as we headed south on Interstate 5, encouraged by the way things were going with the interviews and amazed that Oregon employment might be ours much sooner than we had dared hope.

In the ensuing days I experienced a variety of emotions: *hope* that a job offer would be coming; *concern* that it might be for an amount of money my husband could not accept; *despair* at the thought of rejection by the company; *excitement* as I played with furniture cutouts and made scale drawings of the rooms in our Oregon home; *anticipation* for the lifestyle and peace I felt in my country setting; and later *fear* as my husband seemed unable to choose between going to Oregon or staying in Arizona. An employment offer letter arrived in September, and Roger accepted the position the next day. We moved ahead with the work we thought was necessary on our Arizona home before putting it on the market. He struggled with the start date his new employer desired, knowing it would take longer to provide for a smooth transition from his Arizona employer. He was able to negotiate a later start date and maintain integrity with his longtime employer. We paused to review the things that had happened over the past twelve months to bring us to this point of decision making:

- The way we had come back to look at the river property over a year earlier
- The complete agreement we had regarding the counter-offer amount
- The way all the details came together at the last minute in funding and closing on the home
- The unique way we heard about the Oregon company and any employment potential there for him
- How neighbors informed us of the land use situation next door even though we had secluded ourselves with our focus on projects vs. people
- Connecting with a neighbor who suggested a different yard care provider
- The company's offer in the exact amount we needed, although providing nothing extra
- My husband's expense and income sheet matched to the dollar the company's offer
- The ability to extend the start date to meet my husband's needs with his Arizona employer

It was obvious to me that these things were not mere coincidence; God was the master planner, and we were experiencing His plan coming together to benefit us. My job at the nonprofit organization had already ended in anticipation of our move to Oregon. The income difference was still a concern for Roger. He began to weigh the pros and cons of remaining in Arizona or making the move to Oregon at this time. The question now was whether we would trust God to meet our every need and continue forward with the move. As I sensed my husband about to close the door on the Oregon job opportunity, I felt sadness, disappointment, rejection and despair. He was not able to find peace over the significant difference in earnings and let the Oregon employer know he would not be joining them.

We both experienced the consequences that come from relying on our own strength rather than trusting in God's marvelous provision. It can be difficult, even for those who believe in Jesus, to take a great step of faith and relinquish control of so many unknown details to God. Perhaps it is even more difficult for those who are used to much detail and precision in their work, including engineers, to commit to a future full of unknowns. It was easier for me, blessed with a large measure of faith from the moment I accepted Christ, to see the many ways God had already provided, so I simply trusted in His continued provision. I didn't debate; I was ready to take a step of faith. I struggled when Roger did not see God's provision the same way I did. It all seemed so clear to me, yet it was as if I spoke a foreign language when I tried to help him see what I saw. I was powerless to help my husband overcome his need to see clearly how to proceed when Jesus has opened a door. No amount of praying on my part, pleading with him, revisiting the way the pieces had come together as a gift from God, not by coincidence, had helped. Future details mattered little to me; I knew God would provide for us and looked ahead with anticipation to see what He would do. It felt like we were at the end of our "Oregon adventure," and my happy ending was not in sight. But what did this say about my faith? When I despaired over the job not taken, feared there would never be an acceptable opportunity for him in such a rural setting, and felt the weight of my dream delayed, was I demonstrating faith? The happy ending I had envisioned was not the only possible outcome for us; it was my vision of what God's blessing would look like. The God who had already orchestrated so many small pieces of our Oregon adventure was not limited to my ending for the story. The God who had provided so much to bring us to this point would not abandon us. This was not an issue of faith and trust for him alone; it was an issue of both of us growing in our faith and trusting in God's provision, together.

Within days of Roger declining the Oregon job we reluctantly attended an evening concert we had purchased tickets to earlier. Surprisingly, we were both blessed by Fernando Ortega, a Christian singer, and the rest of his group. My husband was blessed by Andrew Peterson's story about his grandparents starting their home in Florida with only their faith and trust in God. Oh, that we had been able to attend the concert and hear this story earlier. It seemed to be such an encouragement to him and provided a different perspective on change. My blessing came in one of Ortega's songs, "This Good Day." I cried throughout the song, had the words running through my mind while I jogged the following morning, and heard it again in the center of my hurt as I made an entry in my devotional journal that morning. The lyrics are worshipful, recognizing God's provision in all things, while the instrumentation connotes both sadness and hope. The song spoke to my soul. Whether my circumstances are happy or sad, as Psalm 118:24 says, each day is a good gift from the Lord. "This is the day the Lord has made; we will rejoice and be glad in it."

During the sleepless hours following the concert, sitting alone in a dimly lit room, I came to see the reason I could not leave Phoenix and move to Roseburg right away. God did not want me to run away from my husband with the hurt I felt or to punish him by going ahead of him, as I might have done in the past. Fight or flight had been my coping mechanisms for so long, it would have been easy to respond that way again. Rather, God wanted me to stay where I was and work through the issue with my husband in a godly manner. We sought professional help, and at a session with a Christian counselor I gained insight into the hurt and anger I felt; I was afraid my husband would not be able to break free of his fear of the unknown and move with me to Oregon. Nearly a month later, our friend and mentor, Rich, offered guidance to me regarding our Oregon transition. He told me my husband needed my support and encouragement in Arizona at this time, and there would be a time in the future for us to go together to our Oregon home. It was a confirmation of what I had come to understand in the hours alone after the concert. Running away, going on ahead without him, was not an option. We needed to be of the same mind before either of us could make the move to Roseburg. The Lord has such amazing ways of revealing His plans to us, sometimes in the quiet of a night conversation with Him and sometimes confirmed through the discernment of a concerned Christian friend or a concert.

The following spring, we listed our Arizona home "For Sale by Owner" for a few months before putting it into the hands of a professional realtor and received an offer by early July. Roger had decided to accept an early severance package from his Arizona employer and was going to continue working until the closure of the plant where he worked, living in an apartment for the final ten months of his employment. Most of our furniture and belongings left for Oregon by moving van in late August, with the remainder going to his apartment. Faithful friends helped with our two-day garage sale, and Rich came to our rescue early on moving day. I had worked on packing throughout the night, and Roger had taken only a brief sleep break, hoping we would have everything done before the movers appeared if we kept going. Those hopes were in vain, however, with the moving van already there and workers loading items by the time our friend showed up. There was still so much that required packing in the garage, an area that had been barely touched, given our focus on the items inside the home. Our friend stayed with us most of the day and into the evening, packing, getting food to maintain our energy, cleaning up after the van left, and more. There was no doubt God had answered my prayer for help and had sent His servant to our aid. We left Arizona late the following afternoon with a deadline for making it to our Oregon home before ten the following morning. It was a close call, with about a half hour to spare before the carpet cleaner arrived, but we made it. We had yet another example of God providing what is needed, just in the nick of time!

The following ten months, as we lived in separate states, were a time of personal growth and reflection for both of us. We stayed close through phone calls and email communications, interspersed with a few visits to see each other in person. My longest stay in Arizona following the sale of our home there was a month in the fall of 2001. On the return trip to Roseburg, I was snowed in at a Mt. Shasta City motel for two nights. The room was comfortable, the restaurant served good food, and the snow-laden trees surrounding the motel were beautiful. Weather reports indicated a brief break coming before the next wave of winter storms swept through southern Oregon, so I steeled myself for the drive ahead and checked out of the motel. A groundskeeper for the motel helped dig my car out of the heavy snow in the parking lot, and I headed to purchase snow chains before leaving town. My patience was tested during the tedious three-hour drive over the mountain pass between there and Medford. The snow chains stowed in my car were not needed; God had provided once again for my safety and had given me opportunity to develop patience. Following my return to Roseburg, I experienced some sadness and loss of energy as I looked ahead at the time remaining before my husband would be there with me permanently. It seemed so distant to me when I wanted to be sharing the

*Finding Hope*

Oregon experience with him immediately, not waiting so long to enjoy it together. A morning reading in *A Gentle Spirit, Devotional Journal*, with words from Cheryl Biehl, reminded me of the importance of living in the present. She wrote, "Don't rob yourself of the joy of this season by wishing you were in a future or past one. Each season has its unique value; focus on present possibilities, and be content with today. Live each day to its fullest."[10] I chose then to give the future to the Lord, trusting Him to work it out, while I focused on His provisions for each day.

God blessed our first Christmas with Roger's visit to our Roseburg home; just being together there was a wonderful gift from Him. I again felt God's protective hand over me as I took my first Greyhound trip from Roseburg to Phoenix at the end of the following month, in January 2002. A couple from our neighborhood drove me to the downtown bus station and captured the beginning of my journey on my camera. It seemed like such an adventure. One young male passenger seemed to take a protective stance toward me and another female traveling alone, helping me to feel safe at the numerous stops along the way to my Phoenix destination. In the springtime, during a Biblical Counseling Foundations workshop at the local church I attended, I began to see that I harbored a critical spirit and knew I would need to do some work on that aspect of sin in my life. When I saw behaviors in my husband that I thought were not Christlike, was I being judgmental or was I concerned? Had I harbored bitterness and anger toward him in some area and not forgiven him? What was the attitude of my heart? It was God, the gracious revealer, who showed this sin to me and allowed me time to work on the issues that could so critically affect my marriage if there was no change in me. Being apart from my husband for a prolonged period allowed me to focus on God and do the much-needed work in my own spiritual life.

As summer began, my husband sensed that his duties would soon be completed at the Arizona plant, and he began to prepare for his departure to Oregon. The final leg of our "Oregon Adventure" began mid-July, with my drive to Phoenix in my own car so I could transport some

---

[10] *A Gentle Spirit, Devotional Journal,* (Uhrichsville, OH: Barbour Publishing, Inc., 1982), December 19.

of the smaller items back to our new home. The heat was intense as I headed east through the desert of California into Arizona, reminding me of one of the main reasons we had chosen to leave the area. Just before the Palo Verde rest stop I encountered road litter, large chunks of truck tire spread across several lanes, and I tried to straddle the debris. One piece hit the undercarriage hard and ripped out the speedometer cable on my small, low-profile car. Although it was disconcerting driving along not knowing how fast I was going, I was thankful I had not been injured and the car was still drivable. Once again, I sensed the protective hand of God over me during my long journey and knew that I was not truly alone in the desert.

My husband's final day with his longtime Arizona employer, the one he had worked for since earning his electrical engineering degree, fell on his forty-eighth birthday. A man's identity is so closely connected to his work, especially after such a long time with one company, that it was a difficult day for him. He was experiencing a deep sense of loss, closure of one career segment and loss of control regarding what might lie ahead. My greeting at the top of the stairs leading to his apartment, with birthday gift ready and waiting to be opened and a big smile on my face, revealed my complete lack of awareness. What seemed like a time of celebration and rejoicing to me—the combination of his birthday and us finally being together again—felt very different to him. I came to understand he would need time to grieve what he was leaving behind, and I would need to be sensitive to his need. After spending two days at the beautiful Hacienda del Sol resort in southern Arizona, part of it with Eddie and Rich, a couple whose friendship we treasure, we headed north to our Oregon home, travelling in tandem in our two heavily loaded vehicles and communicating by walkie-talkies.

For nearly two years Roger pursued employment opportunities in Roseburg and surrounding areas, most outside his field of education, without success. He was "overqualified" for most of the jobs, according to the people he talked to, and his interest and willingness to do other jobs did not seem to help. The group insurance coverage from his Arizona employment had run out six months after he left work, both of us were too young to receive Medicare, our savings were starting to dwindle, and we were not financially ready to retire. It was a stressful time, and my greatest help came in reading scripture during the long, dry spell between jobs. Matthew 6:34 says, "Therefore do not worry about tomorrow, for tomorrow will worry about its own things. Sufficient for the day is its own trouble." It was futile for me to look to the future, seeing the coming days as bleak and overwhelming, and miss the blessings God was providing each day. The words of Matthew 6:26 provided such encouragement: "Look at the birds of the air, for they neither sow nor reap nor gather into barns; yet your heavenly Father feeds them. Are you not of more value than they?" I knew that I was of great value to my heavenly Father and I clung to that as I stayed alert for indications of His provision. Finally, in early summer of 2004, I saw an employment advertisement in the local paper that seemed to address me, and I applied for a job with the State of Oregon. About the same time, we learned through our church family of an employment opportunity for Roger. It seemed God was opening doors to us that had been closed and was giving us another chance to trust Him in arenas that would be completely new to both of us.

We experienced God's provision again in the details, especially during my quest for employment. When I first saw the ad in the newspaper, it was near the closing date for several local positions with the State of Oregon, so I scrambled to pull together all the required materials. The only way I could be sure my application would make the deadline was to mail the packet in Eugene, rather than take a chance on the timing for delivery of a packet mailed from rural Roseburg. We drove to Eugene, located the main post office, and dropped my application packet in the mailbox just prior to the final pickup time for the day. On the day of my second interview, our drive to town was blocked by a train stopped on the rural railroad crossing on the road that was my only option for getting to the meeting on time. One of the first things neighbors had warned me about when I moved to Roseburg was train delays on that country road. All I could do was close my eyes and pray while he watched for any indication of the reason for the delay. When I finished praying, I opened my eyes and saw the train beginning to move across the tracks. Although we drove as quickly as seemed safe, I arrived at the office five to ten minutes past the scheduled interview time. I was concerned my late arrival would send a negative signal regarding my intention or reliability; however, the interviews were running a little behind schedule, so there was no problem. I said a silent prayer of thanks in the reception room and awaited my turn.

At the time I applied for a job there were openings for two positions, one a higher level of management than the other. Based on the description of duties I read, I had applied for the lesser position, unsure that I met all the qualifications required for the other one. During the interview process it appeared I did meet the qualifications for either job, but the deadline for submission of applications had ended so I could not be considered for the higher-level position. The primary difference to me at that point seemed to be a slightly greater compensation, so I would have liked to be considered for the higher-level position. The hiring manager was able to repost the higher position with no guarantee I would be selected, but at least I had an opportunity to apply and be considered. There was a brief freeze on hiring by the state prior to offers being made to candidates for any positions, so I was left in limbo for a while. I continued to see God's provision for our financial security as I went through the employment process. My past employment experiences had given me skills and abilities that were needed in the positions posted, even though I had never performed the exact duties and had never worked for a state agency. The lay counseling from my nonprofit work, medical background, and management of time, territory, and personnel in past positions all would be needed. It seemed obvious that God was the equipper and had prepared me for the position I now hoped to get. It was a time of excitement, hope, and developing patience as I waited to hear anything from the hiring manager. Finally, I received an offer of the higher-level position and began work in mid-August, with a measure of anxiety and inadequacy thrown into the mix along with the excitement I already felt.

While Roger began employment around the same time, he realized over time that it was not a good match for him, and he followed God's lead into education. His ability in math, a requirement for the electrical engineering position he held for many years, led to part-time employment in the math department of the local community college. A long-time desire to help others become more comfortable with math and gain skill in the subject was finally realized. Ten years later, that teaching experience had prepared and qualified him for employment in the math department at another community college on the Oregon coast. We could never have anticipated this path for him, a man who was uncomfortable speaking before a crowd and saw himself only as an engineer, teaching classes and enjoying it. I stand amazed at the way God can take the pieces of our lives and fashion them together into something so beautiful! "Oh, taste and see that the LORD is good; Blessed is the man who trusts in Him!" (Psalm 34:8, NKJV).

## Chapter 10

## Daily Strength

During the eight-and-a-half years I worked for the State of Oregon, there was ample opportunity for me to experience God's marvelous provision. The apostle Paul spoke in 2 Corinthians 3:5 of his reliance on God, not himself: "Not that we are sufficient of ourselves to think of anything as being from ourselves, but our sufficiency is from God." When I felt completely inadequate, I knew that He was my sufficiency. By the end of my first week on the job, I feared I had gotten into something that was way beyond my ability. It seemed the other managers and staff spoke a foreign language, with acronyms unknown to me interspersed throughout most discussions, leaving me confused and asking for clarification on a regular basis. At the first luncheon with other managers they tossed around terms like "triple A" (AAA) and "dee-sack" (DSAC), as well as names of contact persons everybody at the table but I seemed to know. I felt internal pressure to communicate on an equal basis with them even though I knew most of my peers had been using government-speak for many years; I was embarrassed by my inadequacy. My pride was wounded. It was a truly humbling experience to walk into a workplace feeling reasonably well equipped and come to the end of the first week wondering if I might not be the right person for the job. Knowing that several people I supervised had applied for the position I had gotten and were probably watching closely and judging me did not help as I struggled to understand things that came easily to them.

Time and time again over the next eight years I was convicted of the need to yield all to God, to not rely on my own natural abilities but to rely on His strength. The Book of Psalm has been my refuge in times of trouble or stress, and I found comfort there frequently for

*Finding Hope*

this new workplace experience. Psalm 46:1–3 says, "God is our refuge and strength, a very present help in trouble. Therefore, we will not fear, even though the earth be removed, and though the mountains be carried into the midst of the sea; Though its waters roar and be troubled, though the mountains shake with its swelling." I recalled the Old Testament story of the exodus and how God led His people out of the land of Egypt, protecting them and providing for them in an unfamiliar place. I knew I would find refuge and protection in God in this new workplace and, therefore, I had no reason to fear. The words of 2 Corinthians 12:9–10 provided me with additional assurance: "And He said to me, 'My grace is sufficient for you, for My strength is made perfect in weakness,' therefore most gladly I will rather boast in my infirmities, that the power of Christ may rest upon me." The apostle Paul had been given some physical or other burden that kept him from being prideful. Whatever success he had would not be because of his strength or ability but would reveal the power of Christ in Paul's life. I knew I was weak, lacking in some skills that were needed in my new job, yet I knew God would provide the power and knowledge I needed. My responsibility was to trust in Him and take advantage of the training and coaching that was available to me. I continued to ask about the acronyms as I trusted in God, and before long, I was incorporating many of them into my daily speech.

The state job was my first experience working in a union environment, so I had much to learn about managing represented staff in addition to learning the dedicated, and sometimes antiquated, computer systems, rules and regulations, processes, and daily operations of the office. The learning curve was extremely steep. I found one scripture, Micah 6:8, to be my guide for managing a variety of staff issues during my years with the State. "He has shown you, O man, what is good; and what does the LORD require of you but to do justly, to love mercy, and to walk humbly with your God?" The words were not new to me, as this had been a focus scripture at one of the retreats for women that I attended during the years I lived in Arizona. I quickly sensed that if I allowed this scripture to guide me, it would greatly reduce any risk of workers thinking I played favorites or applied different standards to some. The words of Micah 6:8, written on a small piece of paper, hung in front of me in my work cubicle as a constant reminder of how to navigate this foreign environment. When tensions ran high among workers on one team over a prolonged period, I wrote in my journal, crying out to God as King David did when he was a fugitive in a foreign land. David's words in Psalm 56:1–2 seemed to be a cry from my own heart to God: "Be merciful to me, O God, for man would swallow me up; fighting all day he oppresses me. My enemies would hound me all day, for there are many who fight against me, O Most High."

It seemed no matter how hard I tried to encourage unity among staff and help them learn to work cooperatively together, it was to no avail. The strength to work through these issues with staff came from God, not from my own dwindling reservoir. During times of disciplinary action in the workplace, unrest and agitation occurred among some of the staff, based on the limited knowledge they had of the issue and the concern they felt for their coworkers. This resulted in union solicitation of staff at my office and another local office on one occasion, looking for examples of any unfair treatment or mismanagement by me. Due to the confidential nature of the disciplinary process, I could not provide any explanation or justification of the actions I took to concerned staff, nothing that might help to ease the tension in the workplace. All I could do was provide an overview of the disciplinary process, describing the steps involved, and the general timeframe of the process to them. During this specific time of unrest, I found comfort in Psalm 35:19–20: "Let them not rejoice over me who are wrongfully my enemies; nor let them wink with the eye who hate me without a cause. For they do not speak peace, but they devise deceitful matters against the quiet ones in the land." Hebrews 12:3 says, "For consider Him who endured such hostility from sinners against Himself, lest you become weary and discouraged in your souls." I remembered how Jesus was accused of blasphemy by those who did not understand and how He remained silent before His accusers. My situation was nothing compared to what Christ, the Holy Son of God, endured yet it put my temporary suffering into perspective and helped me take my eyes off myself. I prayed and sought God's protection against lies that had been made against me, and I asked that the truth would be revealed. I also prayed that God would protect the staff members who were caught up in the agitating influence of a few and would relieve the pressure they felt in the workplace.

My burden seemed overwhelming when the workplace stress occurred at the same time my husband and I were going through a prolonged neighborhood dispute, with the subsequent legal proceedings that followed. Throughout the years I worked for the state, God was faithful to provide what I needed each day. He showed me that when I take my eyes off Jesus, as the apostle Peter did in the Book of Matthew, chapter 14, when he stepped out of the boat and began to walk toward Jesus on the water, I sink, just as Peter did. During one meeting in my office with two workers I failed to keep my eyes on Jesus as they made demands and pushed an agenda. My frustration came through in my tone of voice and facial expressions, and I realized soon after the meeting ended that the workers did not see Christ in me that day. I was reminded again that I must face all things in God's strength, not my own. God was faithful to answer my prayers that the truth would be revealed in many difficult work situations.

Management in state offices, especially at my lower level of management, was lonely. Before the end of my first year there I had assumed responsibility for three teams of workers, more than doubling the number of workers I was originally hired to manage. My peers and my direct manager worked at another location in town, so there was no face-to-face interaction with them on a regular basis. Human resources and higher-level management were based in Salem, so discussions on disciplinary issues were usually conducted via conference call. One of the greatest hurdles I faced came about eight months before my retirement. The week I returned from a restful trip to the central Oregon coast, I received a phone call from a manager in Salem doing a reference check on one of the workers I supervised. The potential of losing this highly valued worker to central office had loomed over me for more than a year, and I had selfishly hoped that it would not happen until after I retired. The timing could not have been more inconvenient, given that this worker's team was already down one person and the staff-to-client ratios were not as good as they appeared to be on paper. One worker had a special duty assignment that did not include performing intakes for new clients or annual case evaluation of all existing clients on a caseload. The remaining workers would need to assume more intakes and ongoing case management if this worker was assigned to central office. The change I had feared was now realized, and I had to deal with it. The amazing part to me was my response to the hurdle: the anxious, agitated feeling I had experienced at the loss of other good workers in the past was not there. There was stress, yes, but the accompanying feeling was different. The difference was that this time I had given the burden to God from the beginning. I did not attempt to carry it on my own; instead I yielded control to God and allowed Him to carry me through the challenge. I recognized quickly that my strength was gone; I was running on low after eight years working for the state, but God's strength was more than abundant.

Two months later another long-term worker elected to step down from a leadwork assignment, leaving another gaping hole to fill. The weight of that coming change awoke me one night, manifesting as a vague disruption of my spirit initially and gradually coming into view more clearly. The burden in the middle of the night called me to search God's word, to look in the Book of Psalm, so I got up and crawled into a comfortable chair with my Bible. My reliance on scripture sustained me that night as it had done so many times before. Psalm 18:30 states, "As for God, His way is perfect; the word of the LORD is proven; He is a shield to all who trust in Him." Later as I read Psalm 145:19, I knew that I would find strength, hope and even joy: "He will fulfill the desire of those who fear Him; He also will hear their cry and save them." Throughout eight-and-a-half years working for the State of Oregon, God was my shield, my comforter, and my strength.

I continued to experience God's daily provision throughout a five-year transition from Roseburg to the central coast of Oregon. It began during the years I worked for the state and was completed following my retirement. Roger and I fell in love with this section of the coast after several summers of tenting for a week each time at Beachside, a beautiful campground in the area. We had avoided looking at the coast during our earlier transition from the hot Arizona desert because we had heard and read about the cloudy days, heavy rainfall, and severe winds along the coast, and we feared living there would be depressing during the winter. As we were drawn to the central coast by its rugged beauty, we were aware that the lure of the summer months might not be enough to make it a good permanent location for us. Even though we were finding the Roseburg summers to be too hot for our comfort, we realized more exposure to the coast at various times of year was needed before we could make a wise decision. Our visits to the area during the fall and winter seasons, especially looking at homes during the wettest months, showed us it would be a good match. In the fall of 2010, we made our second offer on an ocean view house that had been beyond our financial reach earlier during the real estate bubble. This time an acceptable price was reached, and we were able to spend nearly a week in our coast home as that year ended. We marveled at the power of God's creation during the stay: sun and hail storms both in the same day, wet snow on the east side of our home and dryness on the west another day while we were cleaning gutters, and an endless variety in the waves, clouds, sunsets, and dawns. I thanked God for the wonderful earthly gift of our coast home, but even more for the heavenly gift of His Son, Jesus. Twenty years earlier I had cried out to God for help, and He responded with the gift of eternal life in the Lord Jesus. Over the ensuing years my relationship with Jesus has grown; my trust in Him and my reliance on Him have increased. My ability to marvel at His creation, at the beauty I see from my coastal home, my hope for eternity—all come from God's heavenly gift to me.

We knew at the time we purchased the coast home that a move there would not be possible until I retired, something we anticipated happening once I reached age sixty-five. My heart was already at the coast when we purchased there, so knowing it would take years to get to the point where we could move there was difficult, yet it gave me something wonderful to anticipate and work hard to achieve. Our first visits to the coast home were like camping in a luxury setting: camp chairs set up in the vaulted great room so we could look at the ocean, air mattress inflated in the empty master bedroom, and some odds and ends of silverware and paper plates for meals. Before long we purchased some items of new furniture, and little by little the visits there began to seem less like camping and more like coming home. It didn't take long to realize the maintenance of two properties would be time consuming and would require frequent weekend trips for my husband while I stayed in Roseburg and tried to keep my head above water with my job. Roger made progress on some coast projects while I put in weekend hours at the office without feeling guilty about being away from him at home. It was in the summer of 2011 that he first let me know he was having trouble letting go of the things he had done in Roseburg, various home and yard projects, and did not feel connected to our coast home. I was shocked, feeling crushed. His involvement in several coast projects and his active role in searching for and selecting furniture had led me to believe he was connecting to our new home. After experiencing the difficult cycle of him letting go during our Arizona- to Roseburg- transition, I was fearful the same thing was about to happen once again. My heart wanted us to be excited together about this new experience. I feared his disconnecting could lead to bitterness and resentment toward me if it continued, especially if he felt pressured by me. I cried out to God for healing for our relationship and for Him to give me the strength to love my husband unconditionally no matter what.

At the end of the year the subject of him not feeling connected came up again, causing us to cut short a holiday visit to the coast. This time the feeling was stronger, and he expressed regret at having purchased the home and questioned whether he had done it against God's will. Waves of sadness, deep sadness, rolled over me like huge waves washing ashore. Days later I wrote in my journal, thanking God for holding me up and keeping my tongue still until He had finished work that was needed between Jesus and me. During the long silent ride from the coast to Roseburg God had allowed me to see my husband through His eyes. Even though I felt let down and rejected by him, God allowed me to love him unconditionally. God brought me to a point of forgiveness toward my husband that I could never have reached on my own that allowed me to move forward. "How many times have I hurt You, Lord? How many times have I let You down? How many times have You forgiven me?" These words I wrote in my journal, the same words I spoke silently to God during the three-and-one-half hour drive, healed my sadness and allowed for reconciliation within our marriage. Our relationship was restored. Over the next few weeks, I began to see some of the reasons behind his reluctance: not being fond of change, finding enjoyment in the present, being a thorough, slower processer than me. I saw that I had been viewing the sale of the Roseburg home as my means of escape, the only way I could get out of the stress of working for the state, and I was feeling trapped and unsupported by his resistance to putting the home on the market. He was not ready to move and leave what was comfortable and felt safe to him while I was desperate to leave where I was; I longed to find peace at our coast home. I finally realized there might be another way, rather than his way or my way, and shared with him several thoughts that had come to mind. He said he felt like a weight had been lifted and committed to look at the financial implications of each option. Once his review was done and discussed with an investment professional, we knew what the timeframe needed to be for my retirement, early 2013. An additional year seemed like such a long time and yet, with an end date agreed to, I knew I would be able to do what was required. The fear of the coastal dream falling apart was much worse than knowing I needed to stay longer in the workplace. I had faith that God would provide exactly what was needed every day that remained; He did just that.

Following my retirement, I began to spend time at the coast for a week or two at times, sometimes alone and sometimes with our beloved dog, Blue. We had adopted him from the Roseburg animal shelter in 2003, and signs of aging were becoming obvious: increasing white in the fur around his eyes, decreased ability to jump up on furniture that had once been easy for him, and increased murmuring and groaning as he settled down onto the floor or his doggy bed. He still had a good appetite and he loved taking walks and going for rides in the car. During one of our coast visits alone, Blue found the entrance to a private path that went around a portion of a lake on the common area part of the community. Although heavy foliage made the path difficult for me to detect, he had no trouble finding it. I chuckled and called him a nature enthusiast as I followed him along the overgrown ground. I sensed his time with us was coming to an end and hoped we would be able to complete our coastal transition in time for Blue to enjoy a few good years with us there.

The coast visits were times of refreshment that allowed me the opportunity to explore the neighborhood, begin to meet neighbors and discover the delight of walking to the Alsea Bay on the beach and returning home on the road that runs parallel to it along the coast. God's creative power was obvious but was especially apparent during one of my earlier visits: in the waves rolling onto the shore during my bay walk, at the sight of gulls lined up on the sand awaiting food at low tide, in rolling waves crashing onto the rocky shore in Yachats, and in the pink and gold shades of the sky at sunset. During my visits

I reclaimed some of the landscaping that had suffered during the years of neglect between the previous owner leaving and our absentee ownership. At times I overdid and suffered the consequences of a sore back and other tender muscles. Somehow, I heard the voice of restraint that came from God and was able to maintain a balance that allowed me to make progress yet enjoy my outdoor activities. My days began with time reading the Bible, followed by devotional readings and making entries in my journal several times a week.

Our good friends from Arizona, Rich and Eddie, blessed us by overnight visits to both of our Oregon homes during the summer of 2014. Soon after their visit, she returned for a girls' week with me at the coast. It was a wonderful time of exploration, going along the coast to check out other towns and natural attractions, as well as visiting numerous small shops along the way. We enjoyed meals out as well as homemade creations, including s'mores toasted over a rusty fire pit, and she captured much of it on camera. It was a wonderful week of friendship and bonding, yet even more. We were two Christian women who had not spent significant time together in the past, mainly brief connections at Sunday church service or for a holiday gathering or at a weekend women's seminar, but never alone for so long. Our conversations around morning devotions were meaningful, and mutual encouragement was a part of our times of sharing. We found we had much in common at the stage of life we shared, and laughter punctuated many of our discussions. We let our "little kids" come out during our adventures, each relishing treats from the local candy store for days, laughing so hard at her s'mores video our jaws hurt and picking straw out of our denim backsides after hours of pulling weeds in the yard. There was no awkwardness between us and no sense of getting on each other's nerves, just a wonderful week together. During the visit she checked the website for the community college in nearby Newport and saw a position posted for a part time math instructor. She shared the good news immediately with Roger and encouraged him to apply. Both she and her husband had been excited about our coastal home, knew that we had owned it for nearly four years at that point in time, and hoped that with me finally retired it would soon become the permanent Keehn location. She and I both sensed that God was opening doors to make that a reality, and all we had to do was to be faithful, trust God, and move forward with the sale of the Roseburg home. Rich, the same friend who had heroically helped us on the Arizona moving day thirteen years earlier, volunteered to spend a week with us helping to prepare the Roseburg yard and home for listing with a realtor. This friend has come to represent to me the servant attitude that Jesus demonstrated to His disciples, in John 13:1–17, in the washing of their feet after their last meal together.

We accomplished so much during our friend's visit: packing a large U-Haul truck to capacity for the subsequent trip to the coast, backyard weeding, applying mulch, moving piles of landscape rock to a less conspicuous area, and distributing twelve yards of driveway gravel. Rich was up early each morning and worked until dusk each night, setting a standard we tried hard to follow. We saw that the three of us had accomplished in less than a week what it would have taken Roger and me two to three months to accomplish alone, given the pace at which we had been doing projects. The community college contacted my husband on his cell phone as we were leaving the U-Haul lot in Newport, inviting him to interview the following week. On the twenty-second of August, the community college made an offer of part-time employment, and he accepted it. Initially he drove to the coast at the beginning of the week for his Monday and Wednesday classes, returning to Roseburg for the remainder of the week and most of the weekend. Although he had not envisioned listing the Roseburg home until the following spring, in 2015, we knew it made sense to shift our primary base of operation to the coast and begin to see the Roseburg home as our secondary property. The pieces fell into place, and the house was listed at the end of August, just prior to the realtor group's September viewing of recently listed properties. We were blessed to be working with a Christian realtor, a man my husband had known for years from Bible studies and church and knew to be a man of integrity.

The amount of work that remained to be done in Roseburg as September came, and the energy that would be needed to maintain two properties in good condition, seemed overwhelming. I recalled how relying on my own strength had led to consequences in the past; God would be my refuge and strength, once again. The estimate we received for professional trimming of two entry area trees, especially if expedited for completion prior to the realtor group tour, was more than we could agree to. The thinning and sculpting of the two maples was added to my to-do list while he monitored the dry rot inspection and well testing that were required by a certain date after listing the property, as well as the carpet cleaning. We were on a fast track after several years of complacency; it was invigorating and frightening at the same time. After three-and-a-half hours working on the first of two maple trees it began to look like we had a tree, rather than an overgrown bush, in the front entry, and I was pleased with the results of my labor.

We were encouraged when sixteen realtors viewed our home one day during their September tour of new listings in our geographical area. Although the listing was late in the peak summer season for home sales, we hoped this was an indication that an offer would be coming soon. We were not in agreement on the initial listing price, and I was concerned his reluctance to go with a lower listing price might be an indication that he was not serious about selling the house at that time, allowing us to be at the coast together. We were soon able to talk about the financial and emotional burden that maintaining two homes was having on us as a couple. He heard my heart and responded by contacting our realtor near the end of September to authorize a lower listing price. In my prayer time, I asked Jesus for His favor in the sale of the house. I acknowledged that we did not deserve it, for we had not trusted His provision for us enough to move forward earlier with a listing as He began making His provision for us known. What price would we pay for not being quick to respond?

When I felt discouragement during the autumn months, I wrote in my journal, thanking Jesus for being faithful to control every detail of a sale that would come in His timing. In late October we received an offer from an out-of-state couple who had not seen the home in person. Our excitement was short-lived as they realized during their visit to Roseburg that the area was more rural than they realized and would not meet some of their family needs. The frequent travel continued for us between our two properties, wearing us down and resulting in little accomplishment with outside maintenance once the rainy season began in both areas. We were able to make progress, however, on the gradual move of items from one home to the other. We experienced the Lord's provision in the amazing way He arranged events at the end of 2014: we were able to pick up the U-Haul two days early, return it later than originally planned, and receive additional miles at no additional cost due to a personal need the owner had; we left Roseburg a day late because of a friend's children being sick, resulting in him not being able to help us load the truck; taking an alternate route because of a road closure on Highway 101 delayed our arrival in Waldport; our part-time neighbor was at the coast for the holiday and came to our rescue in unloading the truck. It was not a coincidence that all the details came together as they did. The extra time allowance and miles provided by the U-Haul owner were all needed, almost to the exact hour and miles, because of the delays in packing and driving. These were details we could not foresee and could not have controlled, yet the modified U-Haul plan met our needs perfectly. I gave thanks to Jesus for knowing and providing exactly what was needed.

At the beginning of 2015 we received two offers on the house at the same time and accepted the lower offer based on the likelihood of that offer going through to completion. We were crushed when the house inspection was completed and we heard the verdict that our shingle roof had run out of life and needed to be replaced. The cost of flood insurance had also increased dramatically since the time we had purchased the home fifteen years earlier, and the buyers were not prepared for that. A FEMA flood plain remapping and loss of government subsidies on flood insurance had made a huge difference in the rates. The flood insurance, something that is required to get a mortgage, was something we had discontinued once we had paid off the mortgage, so we were not aware of the increased cost. The additional cost of roofing that had not been considered when we accepted a lower offer, the inability to share the cost of the new roof with the buyers, and the unexpected yearly insurance cost for them resulted in that offer falling apart. While we waited to hear the outcome, we went ahead, preparing for a moving sale in case the deal closed in early February and securing bids to have the roofing done. The Roseburg house was back on the market just before the end of January. Two realtors showed it before the end of the month, and another offer was made, with our counter-offer accepted on the last day of the month. By mid-February that deal fell through, related to water found in the crawl space during the home inspection that was completed in the middle of a week of heavy rains.

Again, it felt like I was a yo-yo due to the rapid emotional ups and downs, fluctuating between winter purchase offers at the top of the cycle and broken contracts at the bottom. Would a qualified buyer ever come? The market niche for our property seemed to be shrinking, getting smaller each time an offer fell apart. At this point it seemed like it would require a unique buyer: one with financial ability, a desire for country living but without the desire to have a pole barn on the narrow lot, one who would not panic at water in the crawl space during intense periods of rain, one who could handle the cost of flood insurance or would only need a mortgage for a short period of time and could manage the cost of coverage until a mortgage was no longer needed. The pool of potential buyers was dwindling as the long, wet winter dragged on, and I felt discouraged. "How long, Lord?" I asked, as I considered these things. I started to look at the "would have," "could have" and "should haves" of the house sale, and I soon realized I was on the wrong path. That kind of thinking would only lead me into the sin of bitterness or discontentment toward my husband. Only God's word could get me back on track, I knew, so I turned to search the scriptures. Psalm 37:3–5 says, "Trust in the Lord, and do good; dwell in the land, and feed on His faithfulness. Delight yourself also in the LORD, and He shall give you the desires of your heart. Commit your way to the LORD, trust also in Him, and He shall bring it to pass." Reliance on the Lord grew in the middle of my trial.

When I read the February 26 devotion in *My Utmost for His Highest*, I was reminded of the way misgivings about Jesus occur. The devotion encouraged me to bring my misgivings into the open and to confess them with these words: "Lord, I have had misgivings about You. I have not believed in Your abilities, but only my own. And I have not believed in Your almighty power apart from my finite understanding of it."[11] With my eyes focused on Christ, instead of feeling sorry for myself and desperate, I was able to move ahead doing the practical things that still needed to be done and leave the details and timing of the sale to Jesus. In early March, we received an offer from an out-of-state buyer and negotiated an acceptable counteroffer. The new roof was already

---

[11] James Reimann, ed., *My Utmost for His Highest* (Grand Rapids, MI: Discovery House Publishers, 1992) February 26.

*Finding Hope*

in place, and the moving sale had occurred. The house inspection went well, and we anticipated closing around the middle of April prior to delays in their financing that resulted in a month delay in the closing on the property. Near the end of May 2015, we met with the new owners to provide a few "how to" hints on managing the river property and to say our final goodbye to the Roseburg home.

The words of Isaiah 50:10 speak of both trust and reliance: "Who among you fears the LORD? Who obeys the voice of His Servant? Who walks in darkness and has no light? Let him trust in the name of the LORD and rely upon his God." During trials I have drawn closer to God, finding guidance, peace, and strength in His word. As I trusted in Him and relied upon Him, it seemed the darkness of my situation diminished, and I was able to see more clearly. Reliance on the Lord grows in the middle of trials. God is a refuge and strength in every kind of trouble.

## Chapter 11

## *Peaceful Presence*

Throughout my years as a Christian I have experienced the peace that comes from living in close relationship with Jesus many times. It comes to me in the middle of trials as well as during times of quiet reflection. When I faced medical procedures and the death of loved ones, this peace came to me and helped me navigate the myriad difficulties I encountered. When I marveled at God's creation during raging coastal storms, as well as during more tranquil times, this peace overcame me. The words of Psalm 91, verses 1–6, speak of God's protection for the believer. "He who dwells in the secret place of the Most High shall abide under the shadow of the Almighty. I will say of the LORD, 'He is my refuge and my fortress; my God, in Him I will trust.' Surely He shall deliver you from the snare of the fowler and from the perilous pestilence. He shall cover you with His feathers, and under His wings you shall take refuge; His truth shall be your shield and buckler. You shall not be afraid of the terror by night, nor of the arrow that flies by day, nor of the pestilence that walks in darkness, nor of the destruction that lays waste at noonday." God has been my refuge and my fortress. He has delivered me from dangers and calmed my fears. I know that as I walk in relationship with Christ, trusting in Him and seeking Him, I will experience peace.

In December 2000 I received a call from my primary care provider saying I needed to come in to discuss the results of my recent breast MRI. My immediate thought was that cancer had been detected and they needed to share bad news with me in person. There is something so ominous in receiving a call from any healthcare provider where no details are given but an in-person meeting is required. It was with some relief that I soon learned my breast implants of many years had ruptured and needed to be removed and replaced. While the thought of surgery was unpleasant it seemed much better than the alternate option: hearing I had breast cancer. The implants had been inserted prior to the time I accepted Christ, during the days when my sense of worth was derived from the views of the world. My first husband and I visited a local Playboy club occasionally, and I came to the conclusion that my own body was inadequate after watching the Playboy bunnies and comparing myself to them, with their form fitting outfits enhancing their busts as they served us drinks. I had an opportunity to don a bunny suit and got to see how I looked with a cinched-in waist and bust lifted high; I liked the way I looked. It was not long before I realized I was pregnant with my first child and any thought of being a Playboy bunny faded away. I had, however, bought into the lie that a woman with small breasts is somehow inferior to the more amply endowed female. I wasn't good enough the way I was. Four years later, once my second son had finished breast feeding, I proceeded with breast augmentation, cosmetic surgery that enlarged my breasts. It was accomplished through the insertion of saline-filled implants between my breast tissue and chest bones, an elective procedure performed at the doctor's office.

By the time I received the 2000 medical report my perspective had changed dramatically. I knew that I had been "fearfully and wonderfully made," as described in Psalm 139 verse 14, by a Creator who loved me and found me acceptable just as I was and had been prior to the breast augmentation. For years I had been uncomfortable sleeping in certain positions because of the implants becoming firmer over the years and the development of scar tissue that had formed along the incision areas. Now I saw the opportunity to sleep comfortably and avoid the dread of another implant removal and replacement some years in the future, if I elected to simply have the damaged implants taken out. But what would I look like once the implants were removed? Would my appearance be repulsive to my husband? Jesus had provided for me in so many ways for so long; how could I doubt that He would care for me once again? After much prayer and reflection on scripture, discussing the surgery with Roger and receiving his full support of any decision I made, I informed the plastic surgeon that I wanted to have the implants removed but have no replacements inserted. It seemed to me that years earlier I had rejected God's good gift to me, my small but healthy breasts, and I had experienced physical consequences related to my decision to get breast implants. This time, not knowing how I would look after the removal surgery, I trusted in Jesus to provide for me.

The unknown outcome, the potential dangers of anesthesia, and the sense of complete loss of control during surgery are frightening for many people as they approach medical procedures. My own fears, however, were greatest regarding the use of general anesthesia that would be required for the surgical procedure. Even the years I worked as a registered nurse had not lessened my fear of general anesthesia. Whenever possible I choose to have procedures done using only local anesthesia. That was not an option with the breast implant removal or the septoplasty (nasal surgery) procedure that came ten years later; I had to rely completely on Jesus to deliver me safely through both surgeries. My awareness of the power alcohol had over my life, plus the addictive potential of pain medications used in relation to surgical procedures, caused me concern. I communicated my addiction potential clearly to the medical providers, and they worked with me to minimize any risk of addiction. On the day of my surgery I felt God's peace as the nurse prepared me for the procedure, starting an IV and covering me in soft, warm blankets. It was reassuring somehow to hear that she attended the same church I did. Roger was by my side in the pre-op area and we prayed, both of us sensing the presence of the Lord, just prior to staff moving my gurney toward the door of the operating room. The procedure was completed without incident, and I was discharged to go home around noon that day. My expectation regarding how I would feel and what I would be able to do upon discharge was a little off, with the coffee beverage I had envisioned drinking on the way home losing out to sleepiness that hovered over me for hours that afternoon. The following day a kind coworker from the pregnancy center brought a latte and some pastries to my home, along with a gentle hug and words of encouragement.

My first post-operative visit was scheduled for two days after surgery, with the removal of the tight surgical wrap from around my chest as well as the removal of two drainage tubes on the agenda for that visit. My day began with prayer, placing my trust in God regarding what I

*Finding Hope*

would see and how I would feel emotionally once the bandages were removed. I was aware that my strength for the day would come from Christ, from Him alone. My husband, a man who is not fond of medical procedures and pain, came willingly with me into the procedure room. He sat on a chair across the room from me, against the wall, while the assistant and doctor unwrapped the dressing and removed the drains. The snug wrap, placed to help prevent blood leaking under my skin and causing bruising, flattened the remaining breast tissue into something that looked more like a flat pancake than a rounded muffin. There was nothing attractive from my vantage point. Throughout the process I kept my eyes fixed on my husband's face and saw no flicker of negative reaction in his eyes, just a look of love and assurance reflected on his face when he looked at me. That look of acceptance, not revulsion or pity, is still clear in my mind many years later. Roger was a rock for me that day, strengthened by the Lord for that encounter just as I was. Jesus was my faithful provider on that difficult day. He surrounded us with the peace that comes only by trusting in Him.

Nearly three years later I experienced my first cancer diagnosis, something that was frightening even though it was thought to be a basal cell skin cancer and not a more deadly form of cancer. When the doctor said it looked like cancer, my unspoken cry was, "No, it must be a mistake!" A short while later I was able to sit alone in the car and quietly pray, acknowledging that my spirit of fear did not come from the Lord, and to thank Him for being with me through the experience. The following morning I read the words of 2 Chronicles 16:9 in my devotional journal, *The Best of Andrew Murray on Prayer*: "The eyes of the Lord search the whole earth in order to strengthen those whose hearts are fully committed to him."[12] My heart was fully committed to the Lord; I sensed the fear dissipating, leaving only a sense of fragility in its place. Perhaps the diagnosis was a reminder to me of how temporary this life on earth is and an encourager for me to make the most of each precious day. When the biopsy result came back, confirming I had a basal cell carcinoma, I felt relief to hear that it was not melanoma, a more serious form of cancer. I gave thanks to God for this provision

---

[12] A. Murray, *The Best of Andrew Murray on Prayer* (Uhrichsville, OH: Barbour Publishing, Inc., 1996) December 17.

and made the appointment to meet with another dermatologist, who would remove the cancer using the MOHS procedure, a method that allows for removal of all cancer cells leaving a border of good cells surrounding the area where tissue has been removed.

Once more I experienced God's faithful provision for me during a trial: the date of the surgery was two days before the group insurance my husband had carried during his work in Arizona ran out. God knows my every need, and He has shown repeatedly how He meets those needs, growing my trust in Him throughout my years as a Christian. On the day of the surgery I experienced a sense of peace prior to the procedure, during it, and during the return drive home. My discomfort was bearable, even on the day of surgery, and the healing went well. In the Book of Matthew, chapter 9, Jesus heals a paralytic man who is brought to Him in faith by his friends. Jesus healed not only the man's physical condition but also forgave the man his sins. In my journal entry the day after surgery I acknowledged the Lord as my great physician and healer, and I gave thanks for His presence throughout the procedure and the recovery that was just beginning. There has been no recurrence of skin cancer in that location to this day.

In the fall of 2010, I began experiencing sudden and sometimes heavy nosebleeds. It was frightening to have them occur unexpectedly: in the middle of morning walks with my dog, right after arising from bed in the morning, following a single sneeze, and during a quiet meeting in my office with a coworker. On that occasion, the amount of blood looked significant and was not diminishing, so we left the office quickly, and she drove me to urgent care. When I sensed panic welling up, I focused on Jesus and recalled portions of scripture that spoke of His presence, His protection, and His peace. My mind stayed fixed on these things as the urgent care doctor inserted packing material into my left nostril to stop the bleeding and maintain pressure until it could be removed, nearly a week later. Had I focused on the discomfort of the procedure rather than my Lord, the pain and the desire to leave would have overcome me. In February of 2011, I elected to have septoplasty surgery to repair the deviated septum on one side of my nose, a factor that had contributed to the frequent nosebleeds.

In the days before the surgery, I talked to Jesus, acknowledging that He was in control of the entire process, already knew the outcome, and had a plan to benefit me, love me, and bring glory to Himself. I was not anxious, recalling the words of Philippians 4:13, knowing that "I can do all things through Christ who strengthens me." Throughout the day of the surgery I saw the Lord's hand: in the kindness of the anesthesiologist during the preoperative exam, in the peace that washed over me as Roger and I read some of Psalm 91 before I went to the operating room, and in the caring and compassionate registered nurse who cared for me in the recovery area. We connected at a spiritual level because she saw my peace upon awaking from the anesthesia, and she recognized that it was related to my faith in Christ. The postoperative recovery went smoothly, and I was able to leave the outpatient surgery unit of the hospital four-and-a-half hours after my check-in time that morning. I continued to feel the protective hand of the Lord on me throughout the remainder of the day: in my ability to take fluids and light food without nausea, concerning the resolution of a pharmacy mix-up with my medication, in the safety driving through heavy hail on the way home, and the welcome sight of our Roseburg home late that afternoon. My recovery progressed well, with pain managed primarily by Tylenol, the stuffy nose improving gradually, and my husband doing a great job helping with the dressing changes. The outcome was positive, with few nosebleeds in the years that followed and all of them easily stopped using a technique the surgeon shared with me.

 My next medical challenge came in early fall of 2012, in the form of my first permanent tooth extraction. It was difficult reaching the decision to have the tooth pulled, a tooth that I had babied, pampered, and managed to keep for twenty years following the development of deep pockets in the gum tissue around the tooth. Over the years, bone loss in that area had continued gradually and the prognosis for me keeping the tooth much longer was not good. With my retirement date approaching and my group dental insurance ending at that time, I weighed my options and considered the costs I would incur if I delayed. If I waited too long, there might not be an adequate amount of bone available for the oral surgeon to perform an implant successfully. I did not want to give up on the tooth I had spared for such a long time, but I did not want to miss the window of opportunity for receiving an implant; I felt pressured, uncertain, and afraid. It was obvious that I was in my pragmatic mode, trying to find a logical answer on my own rather than looking to God for the answer. The words of Philippians 4:6–7 provided the direction I needed: "Be anxious for nothing, but in everything by prayer and supplication, with thanksgiving, let your requests be made known to God; and the peace of God, which surpasses all understanding, will guard your hearts and minds through Christ Jesus." The confusion cleared, and I was able to reach a decision, scheduling the tooth extraction by local anesthetic on a day in late September.

Frequently during the ride from Roseburg to the dental office in Eugene and while seated in the waiting room, I closed my eyes and talked to God about the procedure. I thanked Him for being there with me, for surrounding me with a hedge of spiritual protection, for giving the dentist the skill needed and for healing me. The sense of dread I had been experiencing diminished as I did this; I still did not have complete comfort in what was about to occur as my name was called. I soon learned there had been some mix-up in the normal routine, with the temporary tooth that was supposed to be there for insertion after surgery not at that location, providing me with an opportunity to postpone the extraction. By this point I was totally committed to the tooth removal, and knew there was no turning back. Post-operative care directions were given to me by the dental assistant prior to the dentist coming into the procedure room, and my written consent was obtained. What followed was only mildly uncomfortable but very quick, and it was the rapidity of the procedure and the finality of the extraction that hit me as I left the office with my husband. We made it as far as the office front door before I started sobbing, and I sobbed all the way to the car with poor Roger trying to figure out what was wrong. With a bundle of gauze clenched tightly between my jaws on the extraction side, saliva oozing out around the gauze and a cold gel pack pressed against my cheek, I tried to assure him they had not pulled the wrong tooth. Eventually I was able to share with him that it was the speed at which everything happened that was unnerving, yet that was coupled with my sense of relief that it was over, as well as a sense of loss. Two days later I wrote in my devotional journal, thanking the Lord for His protection that had been so apparent. I experienced no significant postoperative pain or complications, just jaw tenderness and sensitivity in the teeth on the surgical side. Even the inability to have the temporary tooth, the "flipper tooth," placed on the day of surgery seemed in retrospect to be a blessing. The jaw soreness and tooth sensitivity would be greatly diminished by the time I received the flipper tooth and learned how to insert and remove it. Once again God had been in even the smallest details. He had enabled me to go through a frightening experience, sensing His presence and experiencing His peace.

Throughout most of 2013 I watched a dear friend and his wife as they walked through the valley of the shadow of death as his cancer was diagnosed, progressed, and eventually ended his earthly life. Both were committed Christians, people at church I came to know during my first year living alone in Roseburg. He was a physically strong man, a decorated Vietnam War veteran with a deep booming voice and the ability to connect with people wherever he went. It was a privilege to see their devotion to the Lord and their reliance on Him throughout the long months of treatment and shorter period of rapid decline at the end of the year. When news reached me in early December that he might have only days left, I was in Waldport for a homeowner's association meeting that was scheduled the following day. The temperatures had dropped drastically, and there were winter storm warnings for snow and icy roads for several days in both the Waldport and Roseburg areas. Soon after reading the email about my friend's rapid decline, I received a call saying the coastal meeting had been cancelled due to weather and concerns about HOA Board members travelling safely to Waldport during the storm. I understood that concern well, having gone off the road in a snowstorm in Massachusetts the winter I drove my first car. Although I had watched my dad master snow- and ice-covered roads and hills over the years, his expertise was little help on my first encounter with a slippery slope. I started up the incline with some sense of confidence, trying to do what I thought Dad would have done, and quickly found my car turned ninety degrees, straddling a ditch on the right side of the road. The windshield wipers moved rhythmically back and forth in the stalled car as I stared in disbelief at my predicament. Fortunately, a man driving a pickup truck came by soon after and was able to get my car back on the road and safely up the incline. I was not hurt and suffered only a slight dent on the right side of my car as a result of the event. Telling my father what had happened was the hardest part of the ordeal for me. I felt I had somehow let him down by not being able to follow his example, mastering the winter road, and I was embarrassed at my own failure. The memory of that snow experience when I was in my late teens carried over into my adult years, leaving me anxious about driving in any snowstorm.

During the brief phone call with Roger that followed on that December morning, we agreed that if I was going to make it back to Roseburg prior to the middle of the following week, I would need to leave Waldport by noon. Snow had been falling in both locations since early morning, and the drive ahead was over three hours, even in sunny weather. If it were not for my sense of urgency to be in Roseburg to support my friends, I would never have left the security of my coastal home. My driving skill was not adequate for the journey ahead, and I knew it; my anxiety level was therefore great. My only recourse was to rely on God, to rely on Him completely throughout the travel. Around noontime I pulled out of my driveway in Waldport and began the long, white journey back to Roseburg, talking aloud to God frequently throughout the drive. During the coastal portion of the drive, I had ample opportunity to feel slight slipping on the snow and learned to adjust my speed and gears in response to the challenge. Once I turned off highway 101 at Reedsport and headed east, the condition of the road changed. The snow on the road was deeper and denser, while snow continued to fall in large flakes. It was beautiful, with flakes drifting and piling up on the branches of trees that lined that section of road, yet it was frightening at the same time. Traffic was light, and I was able to follow in ruts left earlier by other drivers in some areas. My verbal expressions of thanksgiving were frequent as I drove eastward. Each deep snow patch I was able to navigate, each slippery spot safely passed was a reason to praise the Lord.

Once I reached the small town of Elkton, I expected the worst of the trip to be over since that seemed to be the highest elevation of the journey. I was wrong, however, and quickly realized things were not improving. As I started up the first steep grade heading south toward Roseburg, I saw a pickup truck crosswise near the ditch just off the right side of the road. It brought back memories of my teen experience, and I gripped the steering wheel more firmly as I forged ahead, reminding myself to breathe. By then I had travelled more than halfway to Roseburg, and there seemed no turning back. I talked to God, thanking Him for getting me so far. I acknowledged time and time again my inability to survive the trip in my own power. The rear-end wiggle of my car was so great going up one steep hill that the car began emitting a strange beeping noise I had never heard before. At the same time, a large snowplow crested the hill and came down toward me; I was sure we would collide. It was God, not me, in control, and I gradually managed to make it, inch by inch, to the top of that grade. By the time I reached downtown Sutherlin the snow was deep in the two-lane road, so deep that I dared get onto I-5 for the short drive south to the next exit rather than stay on the main street and follow a back road home. Normally the back road would have been less stressful. Time seemed to go so slowly, with me plodding ahead mile by mile, my mind fixed on God and longing for my destination, the safety of my Roseburg home. Much of the final eight miles was along a narrow, winding, and in places steep, country road with a sheer drop off on the right side of the road in the direction I was travelling. Four hours after my departure from Waldport, I reached our driveway and the welcoming arms of my husband. There I praised God and gave thanks for Him delivering me safely. My trust in God, my reliance on Him, grows each time I experience His peace.

## Chapter 12

# A Fresh Perspective

As I reflect over my life, both the years prior to knowing Christ and since I accepted Him, I see there has been a major shift in my perspective on numerous issues over the years. The sense of needing to be in control of everything in my life—to anticipate the future and always be one step ahead of the game—had put tremendous stress on me. Once I accepted Christ, I knew that He was the One in control of my life, not me. As I learned of His qualities and went through many trials with Him guiding me, I began to see things more clearly from the biblical perspective. The Creator of all things loves me, knows everything about me, directs me daily through whatever comes my way, rejoices with me, and comforts me as nobody else can. The assurance of His presence, His character, and His great power has changed my perspective about many things.

*The human heart is empty without God. Nothing can satisfy or fill the emptiness but the love of God, available to all through relationship with Jesus Christ.* During my first marriage, initially with just my husband and then one and soon two children, I felt lonely, and I looked in inappropriate places to meet my need. Looking back on that time in my life, I realize my heart was empty without the knowledge and presence of God. There was a heart-shaped vacuum in me, one that is present in all of us prior to accepting God's good gift of His Son. We often attempt to fill that emptiness with activity, possessions and relationships, some of them destructive in nature. We cling tightly to people, places and things in our lives looking for completion without finding it. In so doing, we tend to smother those we have relationship with, sometimes driving them away, missing opportunities as we cling to the place we now know and making idols of the things we acquire and hold so dear. The heart is hungry and cannot rest or find peace or experience true joy, until we have a personal relationship with Christ. Hope is an elusive thing. In the New Testament, Romans 6:23 says, "For the wages of sin is death, but the gift of God is eternal life in Christ Jesus our Lord." Simply hearing about Jesus was not enough for me; I needed to personally accept His gift of forgiveness, as if reaching out and taking a beautiful package from His hands, and let that precious gift become mine.

Prior to accepting Christ, I experienced repetitive, disturbing dreams where I was always desiring and searching for *something*, but no matter how hard I tried, I could not find the elusive *thing*. Through years of studying God's word, I have come to realize that what I sought was the peace and safety of the Lord, like a nestling under the wing of the mother bird. Psalm 36:7–9 says, "How precious is Your loving kindness, O God. Therefore the children of men put their trust under the shadow of Your wings. They are abundantly satisfied with the fullness of Your house, and You give them drink from the river of Your pleasures. For with You is the fountain of life; In Your light we see light." The picture of a baby bird snuggled under the protective wing of its mother, where birds of prey cannot easily snatch it up, is comforting. Sometimes as I sit curled up in a comfortable chair, my feet drawn up into it and a light cover thrown around my shoulders, it feels as if I am nestled in my Father's arms, safe and secure. No earthly possession, experience, or relationship had filled my yearning although I had made many attempts to find an answer. It was not until I accepted Jesus Christ in 1990 that my heart hunger was satisfied. I experienced the lovingkindness of God as I trusted in His Son, Jesus. I had hope.

*The approval and acceptance of the world is empty when compared with the unconditional love Jesus offers.* During my years as a student I sought the approval of my teachers and family members and found it in good grades on my report cards and occasional scholastic rewards, as well as hugs and congratulations from family members when I brought home good grades. Winning third place in an art contest during grade school was exciting and felt good. The small monetary award I received was nice, but the sense of having done something well and receiving attention and praise from my parents was far better. As a worker during my young and middle adult years I sought good performance evaluations and the salary increases that went with those. The temporary pleasure I derived from a good written review or increase in pay was short-lived, however, and I continued to strive to meet some arbitrary standard and await the next manager's proclamation of my value. If a reward or praise did not materialize, I experienced rejection, disappointment, or some other negative emotion. As a spouse, I tried to please my husband and hoped to receive kind words of appreciation or encouragement from him for the cookies I baked or the surprise I planned for his birthday, our anniversary, or some other special occasion. My sense of worth and value in many situations over many years was dependent on the responses of others because I had no sense of my own true worth. The happiness connected with earthly rewards fades in comparison to the joy that I now experience as a result of my walk with the Lord.

It was only as I came to read God's word regularly and participate in scripture-based Bible studies that I discovered my intrinsic value. As I worked through Robert McGee's book and workbook *The Search for Significance*, I discovered four truths that are based on God's word: "I am deeply loved by God; I am completely forgiven and am fully pleasing to God; I am totally accepted by God; and I am complete in Christ."[13] Even if I miss getting the award, the promotion, or the approval of my spouse or other significant person in my life, I have great value. As a believer, I do not want to be tossed about by the ever-changing values of the day, conformed to this world and the things that are popular for the moment; rather, I want to be transformed at a spiritual level. Romans 12:2 says, "And do not be conformed to this world, but be transformed by the renewing of your mind, that you may prove what is that good and acceptable and perfect will of God." My behavior should not be based on the current fads and trends, definition of political correctness, or other worldly value but should reflect the good and acceptable will of God. One wonderful part of my relationship with Jesus is that I don't need to fear losing Him if my performance is less than perfect. I do not have to work to earn His approval

---

[13] R.S. McGee, *The Search for Significance, Book and Workbook* (Nashville, TN: W Publishing Group, 1998), 310.

or my salvation, yet as He transforms me, I desire more and more to please Him and be like Him in my daily living.

*The Word of God has become my guide to daily living, replacing self-help books, expert predictions and the wisdom of the world.* In the Book of Colossians, the apostle Paul says, "Set your mind on things above, not on things on the earth," in chapter 3, verse 2. He then follows with specific instruction on how Christians are to live, citing both negative and positive behaviors. "Anger, wrath, malice, blasphemy, [and] filthy language" are among the things I need to let go of as I live my life in Christ. Some of those behaviors were common in my past and still occasionally pop up, signaling that something is amiss in my relationship with Christ. I know the Holy Spirit alerts me and puts the desire in me to make things right again with Jesus. It is by obedience to God's word that I restore peace in that critical relationship with Jesus and in so doing, I can be reconciled to my husband, son, friend, or neighbor. But God is so good that He does not stop with just providing a list of things to put off; He tells me what I need to put on, as well. In verses 12–15 the apostle says, "put on tender mercies, kindness, humility, meekness, longsuffering; bearing with one another, and forgiving one another; . . . above all these things put on love . . . and let the peace of God rule in your hearts."

As I look at definitions of the qualities I am to put on, I see each tends to define another one, and it is difficult to separate them into individual attributes. For instance, the terms kindness and forbearance, as well as compassion and pity, are all used to define mercies.[14] In one source, kindness is actually defined as "one of a series of terms that are overlapping and not clearly or consistently distinguishable in meaning" with the word kindness linked to the terms "goodness, mercy, pity, love, grace, favor, compassion, gentleness, tenderness, etc."[15] In Easton's Bible Dictionary meekness is defined as "a calm temper of mind, not easily

---

[14] mercies. 2016. In *Dictionary.com*.
Retrieved December 7, 2016, from https://www.dictionary.com/browse/mercies

[15] kindness. 2016. In *BibleStudyTools.com*.
Retrieved December 7, 2016, from http://www.biblestudytools.com/dictionary/kindness

provoked."[16] According to another source, the longsuffering person shows "self-restraint when ... stirred to anger ... does not immediately retaliate or punish ... patiently forbears."[17] All of these qualities from Colossians 3, referred to as the fruit of the Spirit, are found in God and appear in both the Old and New Testament writings of the Bible. I know that I am to live my life reflecting these qualities, and I know that this is possible only as I yield to the Holy Spirit.

The in-depth study of scripture that has been associated with many women's Bible studies confirms and strengthens the importance of God's word in my daily living. During one study, *The Vision of His Glory* by Anne Graham Lotz, the focus was on the Book of Revelation. In the preface of the workbook, Lotz said, "It is important to take the time and make the effort to read His Word carefully and accurately, that we might hear His voice speaking to us personally."[18] Each session included the reading of assigned scripture, identifying the spiritual message found in the words, and then applying the meaning to my own life. As I studied the words of Revelation 2, verses 1–7, I wrote what these words of God meant to me personally: in my thoughts and actions I must love what Christ loves and abhor what He abhors. When the angel of God spoke to the church in Ephesus, He commended it for not tolerating wicked men but held against the church their turning away from God. Scripture is filled with examples of His people turning away, forgetting His precepts, His instruction for life and doing things their own way. In the Book of Exodus, the people of Israel turned away from God, making a golden calf to worship when Moses delayed forty days in returning to them from being with God on Mount Sinai. In spite of God having miraculously delivered them from Pharaoh in Egypt and providing the Ten Commandments to

---

[16] meekness. 2016. In Easton's Bible Dictionary.com
Retrieved December 7, 2016, from http://www.biblestudytools.com/dictionaries/eastons-bible-dictionary/meekness.html

[17] longsuffering. 2016. In gotquestions.org
Retrieved December 7, 2016, from https://www.gotquestions.org/Bible/longsuffering

[18] A.G. Lotz, *The Vision of His Glory, Workbook* (Raleigh, NC: AnGel Ministries, 2015) 5.

guide them in right living, they quickly broke His first commandment: "You shall have no other gods before Me," from Exodus 20, verse 3. In the Book of 1 Samuel, Saul did not follow God's command regarding the actions he was to take in the battle against the Amalekites. Saul let his own desires get in the way and lost his authority as king as a result of his disobedience. In the Book of 2 Samuel, David, Saul's successor, broke God's commandments by having sexual relations with one of his soldier's wives and covering up his sin when she became pregnant by having the warrior killed in battle and then taking her as his wife. There were consequences then for failing to follow God's instructions, and there are consequences now to us when we fail to follow God's instruction, for going our own way and doing what seems right in our own eyes without regard to His word.

In another Lotz devotional study, *Hope in Troubled Times*, the focus was on chapter two of the Book of Joel and the need for God's people to return to Him with changed hearts. Verse thirteen says, "So rend your heart, and not your garments, return to the LORD your God, for He is gracious and merciful, slow to anger, and of great kindness; and He relents from doing harm." It was a change of heart, having true sorrow over sin, that God required, not merely outward expressions that appeared good on the outside. Numerous Old Testament and New Testament people responded to God in this way. When King David was confronted by the prophet Nathan, speaking words from God regarding David's affair with Bathsheba, David acknowledged his sin. Psalm 51 is David's cry to God for mercy, the cleansing of his heart, and the restoration of joy. The words of verses 10–11 demonstrate David's deep level of sorrow: "Create in me a clean heart, O God, and renew a steadfast spirit within me. Do not cast me away from Your presence, and do not take Your Holy Spirit from me." In the Book of 2 Kings, when Josiah heard the words of the Book of the Law, the words of God that had been missing for years under the reign of previous kings, he tore his clothes in response. He gathered the people of Judah together and made a covenant with God in their presence, as written in chapter 23, verse 3, vowing to "keep His commandments and His testimonies and His statutes, with all his heart and all his soul . . ." In the Gospel of Matthew, Peter proclaimed he would never deny Jesus, even if it meant his own life, in response to Jesus's prediction that the disciples would all desert him that very night. Once Christ was taken captive in the garden of Gethsemane by Roman soldiers, Peter was repeatedly accused in the high priest's courtyard of being one of Jesus's followers. After the third accusation and his third denial, Peter recalled the words Jesus had spoken and left broken and with great remorse. Chapter 26, verse 75 says, "So he went out and wept bitterly." God has been merciful, slow to anger and kind to me. What He asks of me today is that I would rend my heart over sin in my life, that I would turn from it and return to Him.

My heart was grieved during the dispute between my husband and a Roseburg neighbor. I heard comments others in the neighborhood made about the dispute. Although I understood the power of spiritual warfare and knew what Roger was battling, they did not. They knew him to be a Christian, and they asked me what had happened to his faith. This broke my heart, for I knew his heart, the way he had changed since he accepted Christ. I feared they questioned whether he truly was a believer. He had not lost his faith, but he had lost his focus, and he was floundering; I did not know how to help him. During a subsequent reading of Romans chapter 12, I realized how badly we had missed the opportunity to demonstrate Christ to our neighbors. Verse 14 tells us, "Bless those who persecute you; bless and do not curse." We had failed to bless when we felt persecuted by one neighbor. Verses 17–18 say, "Repay no one evil for evil. Have regard for good things in the sight of all men. If it is possible, as much as depends on you, live peaceably with all men." Paul goes on in Romans 12:20 to reference the words of Proverbs 25:21–22: "If your enemy is hungry, give him bread to eat; and if he is thirsty, give him water to drink; for so you will heap coals of fire on his head, and the Lord will reward you." In our behaviors we both failed to show the kindness described in scripture to our neighbor. My heart was filled with remorse over an interaction I had with the neighbor's daughter. The words I had spoken to her in anger during an encounter between the neighbor's dogs and our dog came back to haunt me during questioning by their attorney at the court trial. The words in 1 Peter 2:11–12 advise Christians to live in a way that honors Christ and allows the unbeliever to be drawn to Christ by the good deeds they observe in the believer. Anne Graham Lotz quotes the words in her devotional study on First and Second Peter: "Dear friends,

*Finding Hope*

I urge you, as aliens and strangers in the world, to abstain from sinful desires, which war against your soul. Live such good lives among the pagans that, though they accuse you of doing wrong, they may see your good deeds and glorify God on the day he visits us."[19] I had to acknowledge the words I had spoken, and I knew they did not honor God. I had threatened revenge and retaliation if their dogs hurt my dog. The behaviors our friends and neighbors observed in my husband and me were not ones that would draw them to Christ. As I continue to face difficulties in my life, I need to ask myself how my behavior reflects my faith. Sometimes I realize I have responded too quickly with behaviors or words, letting my sin nature have free reign. When that happens, I need to repent and restore my focus on Christ, on Him alone.

Even in the political arena the Word of God is my guide. Near the end of the 2016 presidential election cycle, there were rapidly changing ratings from various political polls and breaking news almost daily about both candidates, making it easy to lose sight of what really mattered. In the past I might have been swayed by the accusations, by the performance during debates, by the looks of the candidates or how I "felt" about them. There were things I disliked about both candidates. For me, the choice came down to more than picking the "lesser of two evils." My choice was determined by the platforms the Republican and Democratic parties had adopted and the values outlined in them. Whether I liked the personality of either candidate, or condoned statements they had made or things they had done, mattered little to me. What mattered most was the difference between the values represented by the two political party platforms. Only the Republican platform supported the sanctity and value of life from the time of conception and the sanctity of marriage between one man and one woman. One party presented a platform of life; the other party presented a platform of death. I knew Supreme Court nominations that would come from those chosen in the 2016 elections would influence the course our nation takes on both issues. My vote for president and vice president was a vote for the values that would be pleasing to God and keeping

---

[19] A.G. Lotz, *I&II Peter, Devotional Worksheets* (Raleigh, NC: AnGel Ministries, 2003) 16.

my focus on His values made it an easier decision for me when it was time to vote.

*The comfort of the Lord, experienced during our times of trial and loss, prepares us to help others in their time of need.* My dad's Alzheimer disease was difficult for both of us. Loss of dignity, diminished cognition, and increasing fragility took a severe toll on him during the final year of his life. My search for skilled providers and resources, management of his dwindling finances, maintaining frequent contact with him, and encouraging him took many hours weekly. Throughout the trial I found strength in the Lord and saw His wonderful provision. Now when others encounter a similar situation with a family member or somebody else dear to them, I am equipped to share resources and offer understanding. The death of my dad's little dog prepared me somewhat for his death a few years later. As I held Peanut in my arms during her final hour and watched as she took her last breath, I sensed that it was part of God's preparation for what was yet to come with my dad. The comfort I felt the night my dad died was something I have been able to share with others during their times of loss. The words of 2 Corinthians 1:3–5 say, "Blessed be the God and Father of our Lord Jesus Christ, the Father of mercies and God of all comfort; who comforts us in all our affliction so that we may be able to comfort those who are in any affliction with the comfort with which we ourselves are comforted by God. For just as the sufferings of Christ are ours in abundance, so also our comfort is abundant through Christ." God has allowed opportunities since my dad's death for me to comfort others going through some form of physical or mental decline or death, ministering to them with prayer and a comforting touch, and by taking time to truly listen. Personal experiences with medical issues have prepared me to comfort others who face surgery, have lost some physical ability, or are fearful about a new diagnosis or procedure they are about to experience. My heart is tender toward those who are hurting because the Lord has been my comforter, and I have felt His tenderness during my own trials.

*Trials and afflictions are God's training field; Christian character and faith are developed and grow in the fields of adversity.* The trials of life do more than prepare us to comfort others. They are the very thing that can bring us closer to God, letting us discover His attributes and experience more of Him. Romans 5:3–4 says, "We also glory in tribulations,

*Finding Hope*

knowing that tribulation produces perseverance; and perseverance, character; and character, hope." The commentary regarding that scripture in the Nelson Study Bible says, "As believers endure tribulation, God works in them to develop certain qualities and virtues that will strengthen them and draw them closer to Him. The result is fortified hope in God and His promises."[20] My perspective on trials has changed dramatically over the years, with the fear and dread I used to experience giving way to understanding, appreciation, and thankfulness.

During one drive from Roseburg to Waldport I watched my husband's hands clenched tightly on the steering wheel as he dodged potholes along a particularly rough patch of road in Lane County. My humor had returned after putting in a grueling day at work the previous day, and I was able to say, "Embrace the pothole; it is your friend." We had a good chuckle over the phrase, despite the absurdity of friendship with a pothole. We knew potholes could cause damage to tires, front end suspension, and alignment. When it comes to potholes in the road, it is really our approach and our reaction to them that makes the difference. As we headed north along Highway 101, we talked about how this applies to so much of our walk with God, as well. We zig and zag, dodging the potholes in our lives, hoping to avoid them, and dreading the next encounter. When things are going smoothly, we can cruise along relying on our own abilities and strength, feeling confident and secure on or own, with little awareness of God's presence. When the road gets rough, full of the potholes of trials and affliction, we are apt to cry out to God. I have chosen to see the potholes in my life as something that bring me closer to God. That doesn't mean I look forward to trials and beckon them my way; however, it does mean I respond differently when they do come and I am able to thank God in the midst of the trial, knowing it will allow me to know Him better and grow in my faith.

One of my favorite books is *My Utmost for His Highest*, a collection of Oswald Chambers's works, containing a devotional message for each day of the year. I have read the devotions year after year and am amazed how a fresh message can come to me after so many previous

---

[20] *The Nelson Study Bible, New King James Version,* (Nashville, TN: Thomas Nelson Publishers, 1997) 1886.

readings. The August 2 devotion is titled "The Teaching of Adversity," and it is a great encourager to anyone going through the trials of life. The scripture reference for the day is John 16:33: "In the world you will have tribulation; but be of good cheer, I have overcome the world." The Christian life is not exempt from adversity; however, the Christian finds strength as he overcomes adversity with Christ. In the words of the devotion, "God never gives us strength for tomorrow, or for the next hour, but only for the strain of the moment."[21] I have found Him to be faithful in providing that strength each time I felt I could not go on, could not face another dispute, another work crisis, another illness, surgery, or death; His supply is never ending.

---

[21] James Reimann, ed., *My Utmost for His Highest* (Grand Rapids, MI: Discovery House Publishers, 1992) August 2.

## Chapter 13

# Delighting In Blessings Found

IT IS DIFFICULT TO BEGIN THE FINAL CHAPTER OF THIS book, knowing that even a significant listing of the blessings I have experienced would be exhaustive for readers yet would still omit many of the blessings I have received from God. Perhaps pausing to look at some of Jesus's miracles during His life, and then sharing how I have experienced similar miracles in my life, would be a good way to begin. The Book of John, chapter 2, tells how Jesus turned jugs that were filled with water into wine at a wedding in Cana at the request of His mother. This was the first time Jesus publicly revealed His deity. Jesus fills my life, not with water turned into wine, but by turning the ordinary into extraordinary joy in my heart: Roger's tender words spoken to me; the sight of a rainbow appearing in the sky; the exquisite sound of a moving violin or cello concerto; a beautiful sunset displayed over the Pacific Ocean. In Matthew, chapter 8, Jesus healed a centurion's servant based on the soldier's belief in Jesus's authority to heal by simply speaking a word. This Gentile soldier who commanded one hundred soldiers was himself under authority and was used to the immediate response of the subordinate to the verbal command of the person in authority. He did not question authority; he expected that the servant would be healed. Jesus has moved me from using God, seeing Him as some magic genie that comes out when I rub the container, to truly believing Him: from giving Jesus my "to do" list of requests in the morning to offering praise to Him throughout the day; from bargaining with Him, saying I will do certain things if He answers my requests, to trusting Him no matter what. In the Book of John, chapter 5, Jesus offered healing to a lame man on the Sabbath, incurring the wrath of the religious leaders for performing what they considered to be work on that day. Jesus offers wholeness to me as I walk in faith: when I cried out for help with my alcohol addiction, trusting Him before I knew Him, He freed me from alcohol's powerful influence on my life and healing me after surgery as I trusted in His provision for me. In Luke, chapter 9, Jesus fed the five thousand with five loaves of bread and two fish. Jesus satisfies my deepest desires, not with mere food, but with Himself: when I felt empty and incomplete in spite of past sexual encounters, Jesus filled the emptiness inside me with His gift of salvation, and took away my awful shame; when walls exist between me and my husband, Jesus accepts me and loves me as I am, and brings restoration to my relationship with my husband. In the Book of Mark, chapter 4, Jesus calmed the raging storm at sea with His words. Jesus speaks peace into my desperation and despair: when my dad lay on his death bed, Jesus and His heavenly host surrounded me and brought peace into the room; when my husband said he would move out of our home during the midst of a neighbor dispute, Jesus calmed me and kept me on a right path; when the civil trial loomed large and there was no escape from it, Jesus walked with me through the fiery ordeal. The Book of John, chapter 9, tells how Jesus healed a man who had been blind from birth and gave him sight. Jesus is the light that illumines the darkness of my life: Jesus's light shone on my addiction, loosening Satan's hold on me and releasing me from that bondage; His light reveals God's word and changes my focus from sin and darkness to Him; Jesus's sacrifice for me on the cross of Calvary puts all wrongs done to me in proper perspective, His light showing me the way to forgiveness. And finally, in John, chapter 11, Jesus raised Lazarus from the grave after he had been dead four days. Jesus brings to life, by the power of His Word, that which is dead: Jesus redeemed me to new spiritual life with Him; He has brought me out of the deadly lifestyle I once led; He has given me a new heart and filled it with hope. These miracles in my life are among the blessings I have found walking with Jesus through both the trials and the peaceful times of my years as a believer.

Repeatedly I have seen how God is in the small things, and I have taken delight in that. Prior to accepting Christ my two sons, their dad, and I were in a traffic accident but escaped tragic injuries. My younger son was still breastfeeding at the time and had just finished nursing at my right breast, so I had repositioned him just prior to the crash to cradle him in my left arm, with his legs toward the passenger door, so he could nurse on the other side. As his father began to execute a left turn, he let out a loud cry as another car that was travelling straight through the intersection crashed into our vehicle. The full force of the impact was into the front passenger door, right where my son's head had been only minutes before the accident. He suffered a broken leg in the incident and was in a full leg cast for a while after the accident. Years later as I recall the event, I know that God's protective hand was over us that day and that a few minutes made the difference between a head injury for my baby, with unknown and potentially devastating consequences, and the leg injury, which had lesser consequences related to it.

During the years I traveled the country roads around Roseburg driving to and from work, roaming deer were a frequent cause for concern. My eyes scanned back and forth while I drove, especially on one section of road that showed frequent signs of carnage from the deer that did not make it out of the road in time as cars travelled through at speeds up to or exceeding the fifty-five miles per hour posted speed in the straight areas of road. On one occasion two deer leaped from the high embankment on the left across the two-lane road just as I approached the corner on my way to work in the morning. There was nothing I could do, other than apply the brakes, as I watched the second deer's back hooves just clear my windshield, allowing it to land safely and continue into the woods on the right side of the road. God's timing, not my driving skill, was what saved the day, and I gave thanks for His protection for me and the deer. Another incident occurred at a different location on the same country road. I was nearing the end of my journey from the Oregon coast to our Roseburg home with my dog, Blue, strapped into the seat next to me. He had begun showing signs of excitement and restlessness as we neared home, so I had gripped his harness with my right hand to restrain him and encourage him to lie down again just before a deer darted into the road in front of us. Time seemed to stand still, like slow-motion photography, as I looked the deer in the eye while it continued past the front of the car into an open field on the right. My foot had hit the brake before I was conscious of the deer, as if God's Spirit had guided me and kept me safe.

Throughout the years Blue was my companion, I saw God's hand at work in our lives and was blessed. No matter where we lived, Blue was a faithful supervisor of whatever project I was engaged in at the moment: sewing Roman shades, creating a rock border or planting bed, trimming bushes or weeding in the yard. By the time he began spending time alone with me at our coast home, he was showing significant signs of aging, and I sensed how precious our time together was. The sight of him stretched out peacefully in the lower level of the yard, dappled afternoon shade bathing him, brought such joy to me. When he could no longer jump up onto the front passenger seat in my car he used the cardboard box step, placed next to the open door, and climbed in for the rides we took as we travelled from one home to the other. An additional box or cooler chest, with padding on top of it as well as on the passenger seat, made a comfortable bed for him. When I looked over at him during the drive, I knew that his time with us was coming to an end, and I knew that he was a good gift from God, one that I would love and enjoy every moment that remained.

On Blue's final day I saw God in the small details, too. The decision to end his suffering, to let him go instead of prolonging the end a few days, did not come easily. It came amidst much anguish and prayers, with many tears. As we began the drive from the coast to his veterinarian in the Roseburg area, he did not want to lie across my lap in the front seat but remained in the back of the SUV. About a half hour from our destination he came forward into my lap and allowed me to pet him the remainder of the drive. Blue had stopped eating and taking medications and was losing weight rapidly by this point in time. Although his vet did not normally work on this day of the week, she had agreed to meet us at her office to administer the drug that would end his suffering if her examination confirmed what we feared. Just before we got out of the car, Roger offered Blue a little piece of dog cookie, and he took it. It seemed that Blue's lying on my lap and taking a small treat from his "dad" were his final gifts to us. We were blessed by such care, concern and kindness from the vet and her staff who had all come to know the three of us well during Blue's years with us. They provided a private room with a comfortable rug that we could sit on with Blue. When his doctor came in, she approached him tenderly and spoke calmly to him, touching him and assessing the degree of muscle mass that had been lost in such a short time. She understood the pain we were feeling, and she sensed how much I wanted to be brave and maintain a calm voice and touch so Blue would not be frightened as she prepared to give him the injection. Once she let us know his heart had stopped beating, I began to sob as I stroked his soft fur with one hand and rested the other hand on Roger's shoulder. The doctor's touch on my back, a gentle rub, allowed my pent-up emotion to be released, and I sobbed loudly. She and her staff left us alone with Blue with no pressure regarding time. Even on the saddest days, God is present, and He is in the details, knowing the pain I feel and providing a way through the trial.

Looking back, I can see how God was in the details when it came to us choosing Blue and Micah to become canine members of our family. Early in our years in Roseburg we decided to adopt a dog from the local animal shelter. My husband's focus was on finding a small-to-medium-size female, based on his earlier experiences owning dogs. We visited the local shelter numerous times and found our hearts touched by many dogs of various breeds and sizes, all in need of a loving home. Eventually we identified a dog that seemed to meet our criteria, and we decided to take her to the outside play area with another dog to see how she interacted with both dogs and people. The other dog was a beautiful black-and-tan-colored male in the fifty-pound range. I had noticed him on an earlier visit to the shelter and thought he was beautiful and of a good temperament but had not mentioned him to Roger because of the criteria we had for adoption. The short time in the play area venture was revealing: the female ran behind me nipping at my heels, an annoying, unacceptable habit, while the male rolled over on his back in a sign of submission to Roger. With one brief encounter our eyes were opened to a possibility we had never considered, adopting the male dog who so skillfully sold himself to us. It seemed God had orchestrated the events to bring the two dogs and us together in a way that would make the choice obvious and move us out of our comfort zone when it came to dog adoption.

In a similar way, we saw God in the details of the transition from losing Blue to making Micah a member of our family. Immediately after Blue's death we took turns vacillating between the "when" for another dog and the "if" of having another dog. We made visits to animal shelters in Newport, Florence, Eugene, and even the shelter in Roseburg, all to no avail. Finally, we realized a degree of closure was needed over our loss of Blue before we would be ready, and it truly seemed the lack of appropriate dogs was linked to that. We selected some photos of Blue enjoying pleasurable outings (camping, beach time, snow play), framed them, and made an attractive photo arrangement to hang on one wall in the kitchen. We had looked for months for an urn to put Blue's ashes into but failed to find anything that seemed right. Recalling a neighbor's suggestion about a pottery shop that had a good variety, we made the journey north on the coast highway to see if there were any options there. At the shop we were blessed with a small, decorative, lidded container that seemed perfect in size for our beloved pet's ashes. One week later, while shopping in Eugene, I received a call from a Waldport neighbor who volunteers at the Newport animal shelter. She wanted to let me know there were several new arrivals, and she thought one dog, especially, might be a good match for us. We visited the shelter the following day, made a deposit to hold the dog she had in mind, discussed the possibility with each other, and prayed, returning the following morning to adopt him. Roger had just finished reading the Book of Micah in the Old Testament, and I had treasured the words of Micah 6:8 for so long: "He has shown you, O man, what is good; and what does the LORD require of you but to do justly, to love mercy, and to walk humbly with your God?" Twenty years earlier this had been the scripture focus for one of the events for ladies at the church we attended at the time in Arizona. The words had strengthened me and guided me during my years of government work in Roseburg. I marveled at the way God's word had repeatedly shown me what was good. There are so many examples of acting fairly and treating others in a right way throughout scripture. God's great mercy is revealed time and time again in the Bible, the mercy He extends to me the greatest example of all. Coming before the Lord in awe with respectfulness and meekness is the natural response for me to the words of Micah 6:8. We named our new, medium-size male dog Micah. Once again, we both sensed that the timing and the small details had been completely in God's hands.

As I read entries made in my journals over the years I see, again and again, the wonderful ways God has blessed me with the beauty of His creation. The sight of fluffy white snow accumulating on the deck of our Roseburg home one January and the joy of seeing deer in the field next door on Easter morning that year were gifts from God. A huge, orange-yellow moon hanging in a dark morning sky brought joy and a sense of closeness to my Creator as did the beauty of the waves and the feel of the ocean breeze during my first beach walk from our coastal home to Alsea Bay. When I saw mourning doves perched in a dead tree, silhouetted against the sky, with feathers puffed to offer protection from the cool morning breeze, it reminded me of the Holy Spirit. The location of the birds and the shape of the branches suggested a menorah, the seven-branched lampstand God described to Moses in the Book of Exodus, and it seemed to me a sign of God's presence. Another day it seemed God revealed Himself to me in the antics of two little squirrels playing and eating in one of the large heritage trees in the backyard. One perched on a stub of broken limb, holding a pinecone in its paws, working it feverishly for food. He began at the cone base and rotated it as he nibbled quickly, like a person working an ear of corn to get the very last kernel. The squirrel, however, was balanced high above the ground, maintaining his balance despite the swift afternoon breeze. His coat, mostly brown with a yellow-orange belly, was beautiful. His tail was bushy and curled tight most of the time, but at times it seemed to be involved in his balancing act against the gusts of wind that blew through the trees. After a while a second squirrel appeared, crowding onto the same stub, looking like two acrobats performing high above the ground without the benefit of a net. This amazing display, viewed through my binoculars, caused the words of Matthew 6:26–27 to come to mind. God cares not only for the birds of the air but also for little creatures like these; how much more must He care for me?

Many days I gaze out the window and notice the amazing way the light changes and reveals things. A cloudy sky displays quickly changing colors: pale grayish blue suddenly imbued with palest rose that slowly fades away. The pink and gold colors of the setting sun change so quickly: one moment the light is too intense to stay focused on the sight, yet within minutes the bright orb dims and sinks beneath the clouds on the horizon. God's hand is obvious in the ever-changing sky, His colors unmatched, and no two displays are exactly alike, as with fingerprints. My heart always quickens at the sight of rainbows and has done so for many years. Each time I see one I am reminded of God's promise in Genesis chapter nine that He will never again bring a flood that would destroy all flesh. God said to Noah in verse seventeen, "This is the sign of the covenant which I have established between Me and all flesh that is on the earth." Some rainbows appear and are gone from sight before I have a chance to see if all the colors of the rainbow are discernable to my eye. Other times the rainbow lingers a long while, and I have time to study it, seeing the colors emerge clearly: red, orange, yellow, green, blue, indigo, and violet. Sometimes the color bands appear wide with a soft, blended transition from one color to the next. At other times, the bands seem narrow and yet have a crispness that makes the differentiation of the blue, indigo, and violet easy. Double rainbows are a special treat and always bring a smile to my face. Every rainbow reminds me of God, His presence, and His love for me.

 God's creative power is revealed in a dragonfly that attaches itself to the edge of our car door in a hot, dusty parking lot in Eugene. The delicacy of the transparent wings, the large multifaceted eyes, and the beautiful colors are captivating. The blues, greens, and golden tones shimmer in iridescence as Roger and I watch, wondering if the beautiful but motionless creature is injured or ill. The sight of Steller's jays squabbling over peanuts I have placed on the posts on our deck brings a smile to my face and lightens the day. Their raucous call announces their presence and continues if I have delayed in putting out a treat for their enjoyment. The beauty of their feathers, with the intense bright blue flashes, and their outrageous behavior as they bully one another to reach the treat first makes each encounter special. Another day I watched two herons flying above the trees near Ona Beach while waiting to carpool with a friend, and their nesting behavior reminded me of the cycles of life. The Book of Ecclesiastes has such beautiful expressions of the cycles and seasons. From Ecclesiastes 1:5: "The sun rises, and the sun goes down, and hastens to the place where it arose." The words of Ecclesiastes 1:7 are, "All the rivers run into the sea, yet the sea is not full; to the place from which the rivers come, there they return again." Ecclesiastes 3, verses 1–8, say in part that there is "a time to be born, and a time to die . . . a time to weep, and a time to laugh . . . a time to gain, and a time to lose . . . a time to love, and a time to hate . . . a time of war, and a time of peace." In this setting where Beaver Creek flows into the ocean and aged coastal trees covered in moss provide safety for nesting, the herons lay their eggs to allow for another

*Finding Hope*

cycle of life. The word *vanity* is used thirty-eight times in the Book of Ecclesiastes, meaning something that is quickly passing. The message to be learned: "Life is a fleeting thing that needs to be savored and enjoyed as a gift from God."[22]

In the Book of Job in the Old Testament, the LORD reveals His great power to Job following much discourse by Job and his three friends regarding Job's plight and the qualities of God. In chapter 38:8–9, the LORD asks, "Or who shut in the sea with doors . . . when I made the clouds its garment." Verse 12 says, "Have you commanded the morning since your days began, and caused the dawn to know its place." These mere mortals had talked so much yet understood so little about the mighty power of God. The LORD asks in verse 22, "Have you entered the treasury of snow, or have you seen the treasury of hail?" "Can you lift up your voice to the clouds, that an abundance of water may cover you?" from verse 34 and "Who can number the clouds by wisdom?" in verse 37. As I read these words, I am filled with a sense of awe and wonder, amazed at the way the LORD has fashioned all things to work together. God asks in chapter 39:1, "Can you mark when the deer gives birth?" In verses 26 and 27, God says, "Does the hawk fly by your wisdom, and spread its wings toward the south? Does the eagle mount up at your command, and make its nest on high?" I have marveled at the sight of hawks soaring over a clump of oak trees in Roseburg, with their piercing call echoing over the river as they hunt. I take delight at the sight of bald eagles swooping overhead as they fly toward the tall coastal trees in Waldport. God reveals His omnipotence to me in the words I read in the Bible, much as He did to Job and his friends through His spoken word. God speaks to me each day through the wonder and beauty of His creation that is all around me.

One of the greatest blessings occurred on my seventieth birthday as I celebrated with my younger son on the central coast of Oregon. Amidst the intermittent rain showers and cloudy skies, we explored the neighborhood where I live and the peaceful, natural shoreline in that area. One day my son took a video of me frolicking with my dog, Micah, and pictures of the interesting logs that had washed up onto

---

[22] *The Nelson Study Bible, New King James Version,* (Nashville, TN: Thomas Nelson Publishers, 1997). 1080

*Delighting In Blessings Found*

the higher areas of the beach. It was obvious my son enjoyed the coastal environment, the tranquility and the beauty of the place I now call home. On my birthday we took another walk to the beach, and he focused on photo opportunities among the logs and beach grasses as I jogged around with Micah. Several times we approached Justin to see how he was doing and then ran off for more beach play. A while later, my son commented on the way the light seemed to come with me, and his pictures were better whenever I came near him. He said it was as if God was with me providing light that diminished when I moved away. The words of God in Numbers 6:25, speaking a blessing on Aaron and his sons, came to mind: "The LORD make His face shine upon you, and be gracious to you." The Bible commentary on the phrase "make His face shine" indicates "pleasure in the presence of God, of an intimate experience that is not unlike that experienced by Moses when he talked with God on Mount Sinai."[23] Another scripture, Ecclesiastes 8:1, says, "A man's wisdom makes his face shine, and the sternness of his face is changed." The commentary portrays "an image of a person who is stable. Out of the depths of experience and understanding, that person is able to enjoy life and build up others."[24] Was this what my son saw that day? The possibility that my son recognized a spiritual reality, the light of God's presence in believers, and connected it with me was a wonderful blessing, the best gift I received for my birthday. "What makes God so dear to us is not so much His big blessings to us, but the tiny things, because they show His amazing intimacy with us—He knows every detail of each of our individual lives."[25] Those words from my Oswald Chambers devotional book describe so beautifully the way His blessings impact me.

The journey I have shared with you is not unique. Many of you will be able to relate to childhood disappointments and hurts, perhaps verbal or physical abuse; broken relationships in adulthood are common and can result in great emotional pain; health issues, including

---

[23] *The Nelson Study Bible, New King James Version,* (Nashville, TN: Thomas Nelson Publishers, 1997) 239–240.

[24] Ibid. 1090.

[25] James Reimann, ed., *My Utmost for His Highest* (Grand Rapids, MI: discovery House Publishers, 1992) June 3.

addictions, surgeries, and even death touch each of us at some point in our lives. The difference lies in the details of my journey, for no two journeys are exactly alike, and in the unique way my belief in Jesus Christ has impacted my life. I journeyed out of darkness, climbing from the pit of addiction and worldly living, filled with shame and hopelessness, into the Light. The first step of my climb was repentance, my turning around from the way I had been going and going in the opposite direction. A devotional message by Blackaby says, "Repentance involves a radical change of heart and mind in which we agree with God's evaluation of our sin and then take specific action to align ourselves with His will. The evidence of repentance is not words of resolve, but a changed life."[26] My life has been changed. Jesus has been my deliverer, overcomer, provider, equipper, and protector. He is a gracious revealer, able to convict, to provide comfort, and to transform me. He is my guide, a master planner, my shield, a refuge, a fortress, and my sufficiency in all situations. His faithfulness and lovingkindness know no bounds. My power to change, my strength to endure trials, and the peace I have while experiencing trials are the result of a personal, intimate relationship with Christ. As the words of 1 Peter 1:9 say, believers are to "proclaim the praises of Him who called you out of darkness into His marvelous light." Jesus called me out of darkness. It is only by His great mercy that I am able now to walk in the light. He alone is worthy of praise, honor and glory!

    If you are uncertain about your spiritual condition, if there is a "heart-shaped vacuum" within you that has not been satisfied, if you are in need of hope for this relationship, this trial, or simply this day, I invite you to come to Jesus. He was born into this world to provide a way for sinful mankind to restore relationship with a righteous God. Jesus died on the cross of Calvary for *me* and for *you*. His gift of salvation is available to all who will come to Him acknowledging their sin and asking for forgiveness. Accepting Christ by faith is the first step of a changed-life journey and the beginning of the most significant relationship in any person's life. Will you take that step now?

---

[26] Henry T. Blackaby & Richard Blackaby, *Experiencing God Day By Day* (Nashville, TN: B&H Publishing Group, 2006) 162.

*"I waited patiently for the LORD; and He inclined to me, and heard my cry. He also brought me up out of a horrible pit, out of miry clay, and set my feet upon a rock, and established my steps" (Ps. 40:1–2).*

# Reader Reflections

WHAT ABOUT YOU?

TAKE SOME TIME TO THINK ABOUT YOUR EARLY YEARS, childhood through high school graduation. What memories do you have of events that caused negative or positive feelings as they occurred?

Have these events affected your adult life? If they have, list the way these events have impacted your life, both negatively and positively.
- Negative:
- Positive:

Have you ever had a sense that "something" is missing in your life, yet been unable to identify what it was? How have you dealt with this?

Have you developed dependency on food or other items to fill the emptiness you feel?

Do you crave acceptance and approval? How have you tried to meet that need?

When you receive acceptance or approval, how do you feel? How long does that emotion last?

Have any of your behaviors, such as anger, impacted others in a way that caused you to feel shame and regret? How do you address the behavior and manage feelings of shame and regret?

IS THERE MORE?

I was an alcoholic whose life was being ruined by alcohol and the poor choices I made. Can you identify with my addictive behavior?

*Finding Hope*

Do you have, or have you ever had, addictive behaviors (such as alcohol, drugs, sex, or pornography) that resulted in you making decisions that significantly and adversely affected your life?

What negative feelings do/did you experience related to your addictive behaviors?

How has your addictive behavior impacted those closest to you?

I thought having a higher education and becoming a nurse would "fix" what was missing in my life and give me an identity. Is there something you have relied on to provide a "fix" in your life, to make you happy?

## WHAT ABOUT FAITH?

I struggled to control my drinking for years, fearing the loss of control, and yet I continued the downward spiral despite all I did. I finally realized that self-control was futile. Have you ever reached the bottom? Are you feeling hopeless?

I had somebody in my life who was eager to introduce me to Jesus. Is there someone in your life that wants to introduce you to Jesus?

I recognized my need for Jesus yet still delayed trusting in Him because of my fear of losing Roger. Is there something that keeps you from trusting in Jesus? What it is?

Perhaps you have tried everything you can think of and have still reached the point of losing hope. Are you willing to hear how to receive the gift of eternal life and how to have a personal, intimate relationship with Jesus?

## WHERE DO YOU FIND POWER?

I experienced freedom from alcohol after I accepted Jesus in 1990. I knew it was not due to willpower or any other ability I possessed. I knew it was a result of the power of the Holy Spirit dwelling in me, helping me to become more like Jesus. The temptation to consume alcohol no longer controlled me.

Are there things tempting you that would adversely affect your life or others if you give in to them? How are you dealing with the temptation?

I recognized several areas of personal sin that were hurting my marriage: bitterness, resentment, and lack of forgiveness. This awareness came through the convicting power of the Holy Spirit.

Do you have a critical nature? Are you criticizing family, friends, or others because they do not measure up to your standards?

Do you have difficulty forgiving others? What grudges are you holding onto?

The Lord's Prayer, found in Luke 11:4, is a model for us regarding forgiveness. We acknowledge our sin to God and ask Him, in His mercy, to forgive us. We acknowledge the need for us to show mercy and forgive others. We ask God to protect us from temptation. Consider the words that Jesus spoke to His Father in the presence of His disciples:

"And forgive us our sins, for we also forgive everyone who is indebted to us. And do not lead us into temptation, but deliver us from the evil one."

Could these words of scripture help you as you deal with a lack of forgiveness?

## How are your relationships?

The words of Philippians 2:3–4 significantly impacted my marriage relationship: "Let nothing be done through selfish ambition or conceit, but in lowliness of mind let each esteem others better than himself. Let each of you look out not only for his own interests, but also for the interest of others." What does that really mean? In our dealings with others we should avoid self-centered motivations, desires, and objectives. A prideful attitude is dangerous in relationships. Showing regard for others, appreciating and valuing them with a humble, modest attitude will benefit relationships. Look out for the well-being and concerns of others.

Be honest—are your relationships more important to you than the things in your life?

How do you react when things go wrong in your relationships? How do you feel afterwards?

Identify how the following attitudes have impacted your relationships:
- Self-centered desire and motivation

- Pride
- Lack of regard for others
- Humility
- Concern for others

## WHAT BURDENS DO YOU CARRY?

The lament psalms of the Old Testament were a source of strength and comfort to me as I experienced trials. I came to know the character and qualities of God during difficult times, when my burdens seemed too much to bear. Although my faith in Christ was new as my father's health declined, I trusted in God. Sometimes our trials are the very thing that bring us to the point of believing in Him.

What burdens are weighing you down as you read this book?

How are they affecting you and others in your life?

Sometimes the pieces seem to *come together* in an amazing way as you are going through a trial. When that does, you often have the sense that it cannot be mere coincidence; it must be *something* more. Has that ever happened to you?

The image of Christ's "footprints in the sand" provided strength to me when my burdens seemed overwhelming near the end of my dad's life. Even if my own strength failed, Christ would see me through to the end. Where do you turn, whom do you trust, when your burdens seem overwhelming?

## WHO IS YOUR ENEMY?

Recognizing the enemy was the first step for me when I encountered spiritual battles in a variety of situations. I believed the words of Ephesians 6:12: "For we do not wrestle against flesh and blood, but against principalities, against powers, against the rulers of the darkness of this age, against spiritual hosts of wickedness in the heavenly places."

Recall a time in the workplace when you encountered confusion, conflict, or general unrest. What was the source or focal point of the turmoil? As you consider the situation, do you see a spiritual influence?

Have you ever experienced difficulties with neighbors? Recall the situations. Was there a spiritual component involved in the difficulties?

Have you ever experienced difficulties in a marriage relationship? If so, recall the reason and the interactions between you and your spouse. Do you see a spiritual influence related to the behaviors you both exhibited?

Have you experienced rejection by a spouse or other loved one? Did it seem that person put their job, success, possessions, or rights above you? How did you react or respond to the challenges of these difficult times?

I clung to God's word often as I experienced times of spiritual warfare. I took things to God in prayer. I found that God always answers prayers: sometimes the answer is "Yes," sometimes it is "No," and sometimes it is "Not now." The outcome was my increased reliance on God in all things. Won't you too develop the habit of taking things to God in prayer?

## WHAT DO YOU BELIEVE?

Robert McGee's formula [My Self Worth = Performance + Others' Opinions"][27] summed up what I experienced throughout much of my life. Can you identify with this?

How has the opinion of others affected your sense of worth?

What measures have you taken to be acceptable to others? At what cost?

"Loser" was the label I placed on myself. The uncontrolled alcohol abuse, abandoned children, and failed marriages left me ashamed and hopeless. My faith in Jesus, my trust in God's word, were what freed me from believing I was a loser.

Can you identify with feeling like a loser, with being unable to change?

"Therefore, if anyone is in Christ, he is a new creation; old things have passed away; behold, all things have become new." As I read the words of 2 Corinthians 5:17, I knew I was already changed. The old beliefs about other people's opinions, my performance, and my worth

---

[27] R.S, McGee, *The Search for Significance, Book and Workbook* (Nashville, TN: W Publishing Group, 1998) 22.

no longer applied. I no longer believed the lie that I could never change. If you have accepted Christ by faith, these words apply to you, too.

Jesus's words, from John 10:10, are for both the believer and those who have not yet trusted in Him. "The thief does not come except to steal, and to kill, and to destroy. I have come that they may have life, and that they may have it more abundantly." Jesus came so that you might have life, even more abundant life. How abundant is your life?

## Where is your trust?

As you read about my trip to Portland to begin the "Oregon Adventure," you probably identified numerous disappointments and frustrations I experienced throughout the first day. Those feelings were a result of my focus on myself and the things that were going wrong. Things seemed much clearer and better when I looked back on the events later that evening.

When you face challenges, where is your focus?

Recall a specific trial. Are you able to see positive aspects now that the situation is behind you?

During the purchase of the Roseburg home and the search for employment for my husband, I experienced the pieces coming together in just the right way. There were too many examples to consider it being mere "coincidence." Still, we relied on our own strength when it came to employment rather than trusting in God's provision, and we suffered consequences.

When you encounter challenging situations, where do you put your trust? Do you trust mainly in yourself? Do you trust in others? Have you put your trust in God?

Jesus told His disciples not to worry. "Consider the ravens, for they neither sow nor reap, which have neither storehouse nor barn; and God feeds them. Of how much more value are you than the birds?" These words from Luke 12:24 speak of God's provision for ravens, birds that were not considered clean by Jewish law. They did not sow or reap, as man could do, nor did they have a permanent dwelling place. If God provides for them, how much more will he do for you?

*Reader Reflections*

## What do you rely on?

Take some time to look back on past trials and identify how God provided for you. You may not have recognized God was working in your life as you went through the trial. You may have thought things were occurring simply by chance. Recall a time when you felt inadequate in a new situation or setting, perhaps feeling weak or overwhelmed. Did it involve a new job, a struggle with a health issue or watching a relationship fall apart?

Consider these words from Psalm 46:1–3: "God is our refuge and strength, a very present help in trouble. Therefore, we will not fear." Do you feel alone; do you feel helpless as you read these words? What would happen to your fears if you took these words to heart?

When my strength was dwindling in the workplace, I turned to scripture. When the divisions among staff, the disciplinary issues and the potential of good staff members leaving threatened to overwhelm me, I relied on God's word. My weariness and discouragement diminished as I read the words of Hebrews 12:3: "For consider Him who endured such hostility from sinners against Himself, lest you become weary and discouraged in your souls."

How do you feel when you consider that Jesus died on the cross for you? Humbled? Thankful? Encouraged?

Consider the words of Psalm 18:30: "As for God, His way is perfect; the word of the LORD is proven; He is a shield to all who trust in Him." Look at each portion of the scripture to get the full impact.

- God's way is *perfect!* That means it is faultless, absolute, precise, and accurate. Do you have any reason to doubt it?
- God is a *shield.* That means protection, defense, and shelter. Is there safety in God and in His written word?
- His shield is for *all who trust in Him.* Have you placed your trust in Him yet? If you have, you will find the same protection and peace I have found. Your reliance on the Lord will grow as you go through trials.

## Are you anxious?

I shared words from Psalm 91 with you, words that spoke to me of God's protection as I went through various trials. I could identify with fears the psalmist named as he wrote: snares and perilous pestilence, terror by night, arrows that fly, and destruction that lays waste. Maybe you have felt trapped, as in a snare, in some situation. Illness and the thought of death can result in anxious thoughts. Fear of the unknown can incapacitate some. What has caused the peace in your life to be shaken?
- A health issue, either personal or somebody dear to you
- Surgery or death
- Destruction of a relationship or career

Most of us have been overcome by fear and anxiety at some time in our lives. How do you respond when this happens to you? Where do you turn when your peace is shaken?

Even people who say they have no specific religion will ask others to pray for them when they are going through trials, feel afraid, or lack peace. They seem to know, or at least hold some hope, that prayer helps in some way during difficult times.

Consider the words of Philippians 4:6–7: "Be anxious for nothing, but in everything by prayer and supplication, with thanksgiving, let your requests be made known to God; and the peace of God, which surpasses all understanding, will guard your hearts and minds through Christ Jesus." Look closely to see the encouragement packed into those words.
- Be anxious for *nothing*—that is God's desire for you.
- Take your requests to God—that is what you can do instead of being anxious.
- By prayer and pleading—God lets you know how to get your requests to Him.
- With thanksgiving—God lets you know the attitude needed.
- The peace of God will guard your heart and mind—this will be the result.

Won't you give this a try the next time your peace is broken?

## What's Your View?

I found hope to be an elusive thing found only in my personal relationship with Christ. The unconditional love of Christ is the source of my joy, not the approval of the world. When we feel hopeless and empty inside, we often try to fill that emptiness with something.

How have you attempted to fill the emptiness in your life? How successful have you been?

How has your desire to be approved by others affected you? How is your behavior influenced by current fads and trends?

As you look back on your trials, do you see positive outcomes that were not evident at the time? How have these trials equipped or prepared you to help others?

I saw trials and afflictions as God's training field. My ability to comfort others grew as I experienced God's comfort during times of loss. I came to understand God better as a result of trials in my life.

How have your character and faith developed during your times of adversity?

The Word of God became my guide to daily living. For me, it held the key to a changed heart and a changed life. Consider the words of 2 Timothy 3:16–17: "All Scripture is given by inspiration of God, and is profitable for doctrine, for reproof, for correction, for instruction in righteousness, that the man of God may be complete, thoroughly equipped for every good work."

How much simpler would life be if you could trust in one source, the Word of God, the way I do?

## How Have You Been Blessed?

Take some time for reflection, now. Allow the blessings I shared to stimulate your thinking about the many ways you have been blessed.

Have you or a loved one been spared injury or death in an accident of some kind? Perhaps you have encountered near-misses when a collision seemed inevitable.

Is there blessing in your relationships, whether with people or with beloved pets?

*Finding Hope*

Do you experience a sense of wonder when you see a beautiful sunset, snow-laden trees, or the sight of birds in flight?

What is it that brings joy to your heart?

I found blessings in the trials I encountered. I recognized a cycle, beginning with trial and ending in blessing. As I went through trials, my trust in God grew, my strength grew, and my reliance on God increased. Instead of experiencing a sense of dread at each new trial, I began to look ahead toward the blessing that was yet to come.

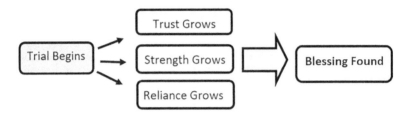

Maybe you have already placed your trust in Jesus but have continued to dread the trials as they appear, not considering the blessings that will come. Have you been focused on a particular outcome and been disappointed when it did not happen?

Take a closer look at some of your trials and see if you can find the blessings. Did you draw closer to God in them? Did you have strength for a long or terrible trial that exceeded your wildest imagination? Was there comfort in scripture and a hunger to be in God's word?

Maybe you are like I was for so long, trusting mainly in yourself and having no spiritual connection, identifying with no religion. Are you wondering if the faith I found in Christ might change your life, as it did mine?

At the end of his evangelistic campaigns, Billy Graham always invited people in attendance to come forth if they had decided to follow Christ. He then led them in a simple prayer that went something like this: "Dear God, I know that I am a sinner. I'm sorry for my sin. I want to turn from my sin. Please forgive me. I believe Jesus Christ is Your Son; I believe He died on the cross for my sin and You raised Him to life. I want Him to come into my heart and take control of my life. I want to trust Jesus as my Savior and follow Him as my Lord from this day forward. In Jesus's Name, amen."[28] These words appear regularly in *Decision* magazine, a monthly publication of the Billy Graham Evangelistic Association, following a message from Billy Graham.

Such a simple prayer, yet it holds the key to a life that is changed. The recognition of personal sin, repentance, and asking for forgiveness all indicate a heart that is ready to receive Christ. The Son of God, Jesus Christ, died on the cross for your sin and He was resurrected from the grave. He is more than able to handle anything that happens in your life. Are you ready now to ask Jesus to change your life?

---

[28] "Come to Christ Today." *Decision,* March 2020, p.37.

# About The Author

LINDA KEEHN EARNED A BACHELOR OF SCIENCE DEGREE in nursing from Arizona State University and a master of business administration from the University of Phoenix (at the Phoenix, Arizona campus). Her professional career included professional nursing, primarily caring for cardiac and dialysis patients, medical sales, and management in crisis pregnancy centers, as well as with Oregon disability services. She is retired and lives with her husband, Roger, and their dog, Micah, on the central Oregon coast.

Since accepting Jesus Christ, she has experienced a dramatic change in the way she lives her life. She has been involved in women's ministry in the churches she has attended, including facilitating Bible studies, and serving as a deaconess. She has seen unbelievers struggle with addictions and the loss of hope, as she once did. She has seen believers not living their lives in the abundance God intends for them. Her goal in writing this book is to tell others about the great power of Jesus Christ to change lives. This news is too good to not share!

CPSIA information can be obtained
at www.ICGtesting.com
Printed in the USA
LVHW040832051020
667943LV00020B/492